"*Dr. Braksick's behavioral leadership model applies equally well to all business situations. It requires top management to focus on and value taking action, not just intentions or words. Whether you are in a turnaround situation or keeping a well-oiled machine rolling forward, the emphasis on behavior is what puts points on the board, builds credibility with employees and customers, and leads to sustainability. Read* **Unlock Behavior, Unleash Profits,** *and it will forever change your leadership approach—as it did mine.*"

—David Moran, President & CEO,
Heinz North America

"*I'm convinced that, to drive sustainable strong results in any competitive environment, you must have the best leaders. Their behavior drives "A" players to join the company and "A" players to stay with the company. The best leaders will help people grow and set the pace for the culture. Culture is driven by leaders' behavior. These are the differentiators that distinguish the truly great companies, where people are energized and accomplish extraordinary things. Dr. Leslie Braksick shows you how to transform the behaviors and the culture of a company with practical and useful information and tools that can help any leader elevate to the next level. This is a remarkable book.*"

—Tom DiDonato, Executive Vice President—
Human Resources, American Eagle Outfitters, Inc.

"*Our most important asset is our people. From my personal experience, using these behavioral tools has proven to be highly successful in engaging the hearts and minds of our leaders. The outcome enabled the environment for a positive cultural change, which substantially raised the bar of expectations for what is attainable, thereby leading to superior business results.*"

—Roland Kell, General Manager,
Chevron Pascagoula Refinery

"The models for applying Behavioral Science that Dr. Braksick shares are both real and practical to our everyday business. By simply understanding 'why people do the things they do,' leadership can create an environment where tapping discretionary performance is the key to achieving business results and creating a workforce that is motivated to achieve their goals. It gets to the heart of what we should be doing as leaders."

—Delores L. Conway, Leadership Development Manager,
CIGNA HealthCare

"In our business unit, we had a very good execution focus, but we were falling short of the excellence we desire. Our work on behaviors, using the methodologies, tools, and processes in this book, has helped us to progress and sustain performance—and we have been one of the corporation's top performers relative to safety, environment, and financials for the past three years."

—Warner Williams, Vice President, Chevron North America Exploration & Production Company,
San Joaquin Valley Business Unit

"Execution is all about delivering on the commitment to achieve operational excellence and profitable growth. Execution requires leaders who know how to influence the right behaviors and foster discretionary performance to get results. We feel so strongly about the behavioral approach to strategy execution, taught in Dr. Braksick's book, that we embedded it into our cornerstone leadership development experience for our most senior managers, and our leaders responded by calling it 'the best leadership development experience of their careers.' They are incorporating the behavioral approach into talent planning, into their conversations about strategy, and into their day-to-day conversations that shape the direction and success of the company."

—Harvette Dixon, Director, Learning & Development,
PPG Industries, Inc.

"Ten years ago, Canadian National Railway started a massive culture change that took us from government-owned corporation to the highest-performing major North American railroad. On virtually every industry success measure— customer satisfaction, operating ratio, asset utilization—CN today is best-in-class, typically by a wide margin. The Market has rewarded this performance with a tenfold-plus increase in stock market price and total market capitalization. At the center of our culture-change lies the 'ABCs' of leadership and organizational change in this book. In the five years CLG has worked with us, every member of management—from my team through front-line supervisors—has been trained/coached to learn and apply these tools. The results speak for themselves."

—Hunter Harrison, President & CEO,
Canadian National Railway

"Unlock Behavior, Unleash Profits is written with the CEO and top organizational leaders in mind. Behavioral science is a technology they can use to change the performance of individuals, entire organizations, and the organizational culture."

—Ward Sproat, Director of Strategic Programs,
PECO Nuclear

"Unlock Behavior, Unleash Profits presents the missing link— behavior—for success in business initiatives, performance concerns, and needed change. It still takes an above-average leader to make these models and concepts come to life, but there is no doubt about it—if you want to be a results-focused leader, here is the missing link to make it happen."

—Jay M. Duffy, Corporate Human Resources,
Center of Excellence, People Development
Training—North America, Bayer AG

"I truly believe this is the key to the high levels of performance we are looking for."

—Mary Ann Zigler, HR Business Partner,
Blair Corporation

"Using the approach and tools outlined in this book, we made dramatic improvements in the performance of our business. In addition, these tools make managing a much more satisfying and rewarding experience for managers themselves."

—Peter McCrea, Vice President, Lubricants & Specialty Products, Chevron Products Company

"An excellent reminder for seasoned executives of the importance of feedback and understanding their impact on people . . . an ideal handbook for new managers on understanding relationships and the impact of their leadership."

—Fran Dramis, Executive Vice President & CIO, BellSouth Corp.

"We learned of the expertise of CLG through one of our board members. Our board was very pleased with the outcomes of your consultation services, particularly with your in-depth report of the strengths and opportunities for growth in our organizational systems, your sensitivity to our mission and values, and the respect with which you professionally interacted with the members of our board and management team in bringing about positive systemic change that continues to benefit our staff and, most importantly, the residents and families that we serve."

—Sister Judith Maroni, CSJ, President, Board of Directors, Villa St. Joseph Residential Care Facility

"I've worked where behavioral management principles were widely applied, and I saw the results first-hand, including in my own management practices . . . behavioral management had more impact than any other intervention . . ."

—Jennifer Powell, HR Manager, Aetna U.S. Healthcare

"Dr. Braksick's book does the nearly impossible! It explains behavior in a way that is technically and psychologically accurate, but also useful and actionable."

—George Krock, Retired Director, HR Planning & Development, PPG Industries, Inc.

"The principles and tools of Behavioral Science that Dr. Braksick describes so clearly and comprehensively in this book have helped us improve behaviors—especially leadership behaviors—for better performance throughout the company."

—Jim Tighe, Former Manager, Corporate Quality, Chevron Corporation

"Dr. Braksick's articulate, proven prescriptions for analyzing, shaping, and measuring one's behavior and for coaching colleagues and family are vital elements for achieving stretch objectives in our meritocratic society."

—Phillip W. Heston, Retired VP, Citibank, N.A.

*"**Unlock Behavior, Unleash Profits** was an epiphany for me. I have worked for years in Human Resources and Training, yet I was never exposed to the Behavioral Science underlying why people perform or choose not to act. Now I understand how consequences drive everything we do. These principles have been very useful in both my professional and personal life."*

—Phil Sprick, Strategy Execution Coach, Stewart Enterprises

"Count me among those who hounded Dr. Braksick to write this book! It is clearly needed to unleash each company's potential by explicitly addressing behavioral issues. It is a thorough, practical guide on applying Behavioral Science to achieve important business results."

—Jack C. Beers, Retired Managing Consultant, Chevron Chemical Company

"The process you guided us through helped our organization grow. The biggest benefit was the development of our managers, who learned behavior analysis, giving them a new problem-solving structure to follow. They also learned ways of coaching, the value of positive encouragement, and acquired key tools for positively impacting employees' behavior."

—Mary Murray, Executive Director,
Villa St. Joseph Residential Care Facility

"The skill-building guidelines in the art of giving feedback, integrated with Behavioral Science, increase my understanding of people. Dr. Braksick's book helps me make my personal and job worlds better places."

—David Tarnowski, Senior Electrical Engineer,
Whirlpool Corporation

"Having a common set of tools and language in our corporation sets the foundation for productivity. Our leaders are developing the skills to focus on behaviors that drive results—those which have a direct impact on the bottom line. Behavioral-based coaching introduced an invigorating and revitalizing method for training our leaders to be the best in the business!"

—Rhonda J. Hollabaugh, Fulfillment Training Manager,
Blair Corporation

Unlock Behavior, Unleash Profits

Developing Leadership Behavior
That Drives Profitability
in Your Organization

LESLIE WILK BRAKSICK, PH.D.

Second Edition

McGraw-Hill

New York Chicago San Francisco Lisbon London
Madrid Mexico City Milan New Delhi San Juan
Seoul Singapore Sidney Toronto

ISBN-13: 978-0-07-149067-2
ISBN-10: 0-07-149067-1

Text set in Sabon and Univers by Janet Coen, CLG Creative Services. Graphics, cover, and book design by Scattaregia Design.

Dr. Braksick has assigned all royalties from this book to the Sydney Leigh Braksick Heart Fund at Children's Hospital of Pittsburgh Foundation.

Children's
Hospital of Pittsburgh
Foundation

More information:
412–586–6310 • www.givetochildrens.org

Contents

Foreword to the Second Edition

WHEN I FIRST MET LESLIE IN 1998, I was corporate officer and President of the technology company of a Fortune 10 corporation. I was immediately struck by her intense interest in the details of our business—after all, we were getting together to talk about creating behavioral change. And it is this marriage between her deep understanding of Behavioral Science, and her knowledge of the business world, that characterizes her work, and this book.

Behavioral Science can be as complex as the human condition itself, but like any complex system, human behavior is driven by a few simple principles. This book is about that simplicity, and how to harness it for greater productivity. It is about doing, and the practical implications in a business context.

Behavior is probably the most powerful, and yet least understood aspect of leadership—the pivotal link between strategy and results. In retrospect, it is sobering to reflect that for most of my own career, I had assumed that with clear objectives and thoughtful strategy, the behaviors required for effective execution would follow automatically.

It was only when faced with the challenge of fundamentally refocusing a large technology organization that I started to look for answers to questions about the changes in behavior that would be required, and how they could be effectively sustained.

CLG's approach, which is the subject of this book, uses simple analytical techniques to pinpoint critical behaviors, and identify the antecedents and consequences that cause these behaviors to be sustained. The emphasis on coaching and feedback, and the techniques this book employs to encourage specific behaviors, have huge collateral benefits in creating a positive, feedback-driven culture across the whole organization.

The book draws on practical examples from CLG's experience with its blue-ribbon roster of clients. These enliven and transform what would otherwise be a dry behavioral text into an experience the reader can share. Most importantly, the process starts and ends with business purpose.

I have worked with Leslie over a period of several years and have experienced first-hand the transformation of a large organization using these concepts. Their impact is profound, and the business results impressive. It is now refreshing to find a book that deals with this subject in such simple and practical terms. The reader will discover that the essence of creating fundamental organizational change is as simple as "ABC"!

Let me add my thanks to Leslie for her insights, which have had such a positive influence on the working lives of so many like me.

Grand Cayman,   W.R.K. Innes, D. Eng.
Cayman Islands
February, 2007

Dr. Innes dedicated nearly four decades to a Fortune 10 company, performing international, executive, and leadership roles.

CLG (The Continuous Learning Group), co-founded by the author of this book, is a consultancy that specializes in strategy execution through the application of Behavioral Science.

Preface to the Second Edition

THIS BOOK IS FOR LEADERS: business managers and executives, parents, clergy, coaches, administrators, HR professionals, teachers—anyone who has influence over the actions of others—anyone who wants to make a difference in their lifetime—anyone who is blessed with the responsibility of leading others.

As leaders, our behavior profoundly influences those around us. Thus, it is our responsibility to equip ourselves to fulfill our leadership role well. Leadership is something you cannot delegate.

I wrote *Unlock Behavior, Unleash Profits* for leaders who are interested in understanding why people do what they do—and who want to make the workplace and the organizations to which they belong positive, productive, and profitable for all involved.

I chose to update the original book (2000) with this revised edition because I saw such dramatic changes in the world and in the workplace over the past seven years—with many more changes right around the corner.

For the first time in our lifetimes, our workforce will soon be dominated by a generation of people who are not committed first and foremost to the companies for which they work. They are a workforce that will work, on average, for six different companies in their lifetime. They will move company-to-company for a promotion or something more that they want, regardless of their satisfaction levels with their current employer. However, they will not relocate their family for a promotion, unless it is desired by the entire family.

This is a generation that is seeking reciprocity in their employee-employer relationship—and they expect to be well-led and developed during their tenure with a company. They are well-educated, well-traveled, and will have their pick of where they'd like to work. *For the first time in our lifetimes, there will be greater need for managers/leaders than there will be people available to fill those positions.*

All of these things, on top of the amazing pace of change and technology advances, and the ever-increasing competition and pressure from Wall Street, put tremendous pressure on companies to be more thoughtful in how they select, lead, manage, and retain talent. Leaders in these organizations have to be much more thoughtful about the role of people and behavior.

This book is all about leadership—and about behavior—and the science that underlies what great leaders need to engage fully: the behaviors of the organizations they lead. In this edition, the case studies and stories are plentiful—and the honesty of leaders interviewed is humbling and educational.

Choose to maximize your effectiveness as a leader, manager, parent, spouse, partner, colleague, and friend. Read this book—and put the concepts into practice in your own life. There is no greater personal reward than knowing you have *unlocked behavior and unleashed profits*—in your life, or in the lives of others. Go for it. It will change your life.

Acknowledgments

THERE ARE MANY who have played a role in supporting me and the writing of this book. I am so grateful to you all!

The behavioral scientists who have influenced my thinking and work include Drs. B.F. Skinner, Tom Gilbert, Geary Rummler, Dale Brethower, Bill Redmon, Bill Hopkins, Paul Brown, Julie Smith, Alyce Dickinson, and Aubrey Daniels. In particular, I recognize Bill Redmon for his friendship, wisdom, support, and companionship on this long journey. Paul Brown, better than any other, role-modeled the simplifying and teaching of the tools in a way that was fun and engaging to the learners. Paul's work influenced how I approached this second edition. Julie Smith continues her invaluable role in the field of behavior analysis by codifying the less-talked-about aspects of implementing change and of being change-resilient. She also continues her invaluable role as my friend and fellow journeywoman, for which I feel blessed.

I am grateful—always—for the thinking and work of my colleagues at CLG. Their work and advancement of CLG's offerings are featured in this second edition. In different ways, each member of the firm has contributed to this book coming into being. In particular, I recognize Galen for the cold water when needed—and Ned, Julie, Tracy, and Galen for the helpful unsticking when I was stuck.

Specifically, I would like to thank and recognize those consultants who reviewed all or part of the manuscript and provided helpful input: Carolina Aguilera, Amy Armitage, John Burden, Karen Bush, Paula Butte, Kathy Callahan, Charles Carnes, Brenda Chartrand, Laura Cochran, Brian Cole, John Dale, Francisco Gomez, Jim Hillgren, Steve Jacobs, Judy Johnson, Laura Methot, Annemarie Michaud, Ned Morse,

Hilary Potts, Galen Reese, Manny Rodríguez, Richard Sandrock, Julie Smith, Denny Sullivan, and Tracy Thurkow.

In addition, I would like to thank other members of the CLG Team whose tireless dedication to our clients continues to benefit them and advance the application of Behavioral Science applied to business: Amy Ayers, Frank Berardi, Lee Berti, Heinz Buschang, Marcia Corbett, Frank DeVine, Jane DeVries, Paul Fjelsta, Bob Gargani, Elizabeth Gibson, Gail Goodrich-Harwood, Karen Gorman, Nancy Grable, George Greanias, Vicki Hathorn, Jack Hinzman, Susan Hoberecht, Lois Hogan, Jennifer Howard, Vince Johnson, Will Jones, Pat Keith, Susan Kilgore, Ann Linn, Jean-Yves Lord, Pam Magoon, Travis McNeal, Jacques Michaud, Courtney Mills, Tim Nolan, Steve Quesnelle, Jerry Remillard, Bob Riskin, Bridget Russell, Susan Shaw, Richard Sleece, Gloria Vick, and Tom Zwicker.

I will always feel that one of my greatest fortunes has been the clients who have entrusted me with their organizations and their leadership success. Brian Baker, Darry Callahan, Rob Canizares, Tom DiDonato, Bill Innes, Bill Johnson, Alan Kelly, Jerry Kohlenberger, Mark Kutner, Brian McNeill, Dave Moran, LeAnn Nealz, John Peppercorn, Steve Simon, and others—enabled me to practice my craft where it made a difference.

I extend much thanks to the CLG clients who were excited to have their stories told in this book and in other CLG publications: Paul Allinson, Brian Baker, Tom DiDonato, Hunter Harrison, Don Hamm, Roland Kell, Dave Moran, Mary Murray, Bill Redmon, Gordon Trafton, Scott Storrer, and Warner Williams.

Client feedback is always valuable, and Don Hamm, Matt Knight, and Phil Sprick provided early reads and feedback that were most helpful.

The hands which helped to produce this book were many and invaluable. My development editor, Fred Schroyer, was once again my partner in crime from start to finish. I hope never to have to write a book without Fred on the other end of my email. His talents are many; his focus and encouragement were tireless; and his friendship and support meant the most. Special thanks to Jim Scattaregia for the beautiful cover design and upgraded graphics throughout the book. And thanks to Jamie Berdine, who kept things organized and moving forward throughout the writing process—her support of my work continues to be invaluable.

The talents of Janet Coen in composition and layout, Martin Verna in design, Daryl Clemmens in capturing our client stories, Nancy Gover in copy editing, Leah McAllister in research, and Donna Kullman and Elisha Dew in proofreading were terrifically helpful and deeply appreciated.

My special thanks go to my publisher, Mary Glenn, for her support, enthusiasm, and continuing guidance, and to the expert production staff of McGraw-Hill.

The love and support from my family and friends was endless. Matt is my soulmate and partner in everything I do well. Our daughter Madeleine is my source of empathy and encouragement, and our son Austin is the cheerleader we all need in life. My parents Herb and Connie Wilk and Norm and Carol Braksick were always there with a supportive comment and hug. Nicole and David, Michele and Donald, Karen and Jared, Barry, Amy, and Marv reminded me of the extended family support that was never far from reach.

The Grapes (Maribeth, Liz, Beth, Michele, Liz, Corinne, Terri, and always Kathy) are in my heart and soul. Gail, Beth, Elyse, Court, Kate, Renee, Mary, and Beth are the A-team most people only dream about ever having in their lives.

And finally, I recognize and thank the Children's Hospital of Pittsburgh, which is the sole recipient of all royalties from the sale of this book. The physicians and nurses at Children's perform miracles every single day. It is a very special place—a place you pray you never find yourself—but a place for which you give thanks when the events of life put you there. I will always be indebted for the skillful hands, brilliant minds, and warm hearts that comprise the team at Children's Hospital of Pittsburgh.

Dedication

To Mom and Dad for my beginnings . . .

To Matt, Austin, and Madeleine for my every day and every night . . .

And to the CLG Team, for making a difference for so many, by all you do and are . . .

Cheers!

Great Execution Depends on—*Behavior*

"I was CEO almost three years before I really had my arms around the role. I had been deluded into thinking I was doing a good job, because I was directing things. I had no role model for the 'soft stuff' that the CEO was supposed to do.

"The biggest challenges were much less about business and strategy—but rather about providing leadership in the right way; knowing what to get involved in and what not to; and understanding the implications of what I said and did. I grossly underestimated the importance of my own leadership behaviors, and of coaching and encouraging other leaders.

"It became clear that, if I kept doing the same stuff, I would get the same results. I needed to change, to do things differently. It's hard to learn new behaviors when you have a big ego and a strong track record of success!

"Four years ago, I would have called myself a good CEO, because back then, I didn't know better. Today I know better—and can honestly say: I am a very good CEO."

—Chairman & CEO, Fortune 100 Company

L EADERS WANT TO BE SUCCESSFUL—not just through their own eyes, but in the eyes of others. And by definition, the success of leaders is determined by their ability to get things done through others. In the opening quote, what the leader learned that made him a "very good CEO" was that *his behavior was the catalyst that could either switch off or turn on the right behaviors in his organization* to achieve their key business goals.

If you're like most leaders, you want to make a difference in this world and in your lifetime, and you are likely involved in a variety of important leadership roles where what you do and say really matters. I also imagine that experience has taught you the hard realities of the workplace: leaders do not always lead well. Good people do not always work hard. High performers do not always get paid more. Angry people do not always quit their jobs and go elsewhere. Great places to work may not be profitable and may not survive. And fairness seldom operates at work.

Reading this book and mastering its contents will help you understand why people do what they do—and how to "unlock" and dramatically change your own leadership behavior—to accelerate your progress to maximum effectiveness. This book will help demystify why others do what they do (or don't do what they are supposed to). You will learn how to focus your own leadership behaviors and those of others.

WHY IS THIS LEADERSHIP BOOK UNIQUE?

There are thousands of leadership books out there. What makes this one different? Most leaders have never learned a practical approach to understanding why people do and say the things they do—and how to "unlock" their behaviors to bring out the best in everyone, which leads to superior performance—both individually and organizationally.

And in any organization, *nothing can improve until people change their behavior.* There is a science devoted to behavior, and that science underlies what is taught and described in this book. It will seem simple and it is easy to learn, but when put into practice it becomes a profound, life-changing approach to leadership.

THE SCIENCE OF BEHAVIOR—AND THE LINK TO RESULTS

The science of behavior relies on honest, direct, useful communication, based on objective observation. It is very much a teaching and coaching approach, in which the leader's goal is the success of every employee. The science is easily learned and is replicable.

While many leaders may find the idea of "soft" people skills too squishy, the empirical nature of Behavioral Science provides the tools to cut through many soft factors, such as personality and motivation. For a so-called "soft" people skill, the science of behavior is really quite hard.

Part of the rigor of Behavioral Science is that it gives you an early indicator (leading indicator) of whether you are on target. When you select the right behaviors to measure, you gain the ability to predict—early— whether you will achieve results, and if not, Behavioral Science helps you correct the course.

> **The Science of Behavior. . .**
>
> explains *behavior*: why we do what we do, say what we say, or don't act at all. Behavioral Science has the same properties as other natural sciences like chemistry and biology: careful observation, data collection, reliability of occurrence, replicability, measurability, laws, and rigor.
>
> B. F. Skinner, Ph.D., has been the focal point for modern-day behavioral scientific philosophy and research, which began in the 1920s. Since his day, the science has matured through eight decades of research, and today we focus on its application in organizations.
>
> The behavioral approach is now the most powerful and enduring way to achieve sustainable business results. Thus, we need its reliable, replicable technology for managing behavior and implementing change.

When you implement an organizational change, you need measures of success. In business, the dominant measure is P&L, but P&L comes too late—you need the early indicator that behavioral measurement enables. The unlocking of specific behavior that is linked to end results clearly correlates to the unleashing of profits, as our company has shown in decades of client engagements.

SO, WHY THE TITLE: "UNLOCK BEHAVIOR, UNLEASH PROFITS"?

In so many organizations, people's behavior is "locked." This means that their behavior is constrained by cultural norms and people systems. These constraints act to keep people doing their jobs at *minimum* acceptable levels of performance. People in such performance-constrained organizations—whether a team, a department, or the entire corporation—feel "locked" or stuck, and their performance is compromised as a result. Often, this minimum performance becomes acceptable and expected, and so the organization chugs along—adequately.

However, locked behavior becomes an insurmountable problem when the organization goes to implement a new strategy or to make a big change that requires people to alter how they work—to exhibit new behaviors to get new performance. These locked behaviors become big obstacles to implementation, keeping people from embracing the new way.

But there is good news: anyone who heeds the lessons in this book can become one of those great leaders who implements change well. You can help your people become completely engaged in "new ways" if you understand behavior, and care enough to lead your people well and coach others to success.

So, the purpose of this book is to reveal how to *unlock behaviors* in your organization, so you can *unleash profits*—not only monetary, but also the vast wealth of talent and capability that is trapped within the people in your organization.

HOW DOES "LOCKING" HAPPEN?

Behaviors become locked as the result of unintended consequences—despite leaders' good intentions. Many organizations unwittingly reward the wrong behaviors and discourage the right behaviors, thus undermining their hard work for success. For example:

> One client needed *strong teamwork* across salespeople in different business units to drive top-line growth, cross-selling,

and meet the new purchasing and distribution requirements of their largest customer. But, the company did not alter its sales incentive system—which was tied to *individual performance* only—thus discouraging any acts of teamwork or collaboration.

The results were competition between business units and finger-pointing among individuals. Top-line growth was negatively impacted, and customer requirements were not met. What teamwork?

The company had unintentionally locked the employees' behavior and leashed profits by not altering sales incentives (consequences) tied to their behavior. They expected people to do the right thing no matter what—but failed to realize that the company also had an obligation to align its reward structure with what it was asking of its employees.

Often the conflict is more subtle: it is the experience employees have when they observe the difference between an organization's vision and stated values, and what they see actually practiced and encouraged every day. This clash between words and actions weakens commitment and causes distrust of leaders and of the company as a whole.

This is where unintended consequences begin, driving performance down, not up. The organization gets less than what its individuals are capable of giving—and the employees experience less satisfaction from a work environment that has the potential to be so much better. When an organization locks its people's behaviors, everyone suffers—individual employees, managers, top leaders, customers, and shareholders.

The thing I want to inspire and excite you with is that employees' discretionary performance can be unlocked by leaders . . .

. . . who understand the effect of unintended consequences on their people, and how to change that . . .

. . . and who understand how to positively motivate the behaviors of others to get things accomplished.

You will get back from employees (and others) the very level of performance that your leadership actions produce. This cause-and-effect relationship between your actions and people's response is almost entirely under your control. You can become a great leader if you want to, and are willing to learn and use the methods in this book. The choice is yours.

"DISCRETIONARY PERFORMANCE" — TAPPING THE POWER WITHIN US ALL

Discretionary performance is that extra level of performance we exert when we <u>want</u> to do something, as opposed to when we <u>have</u> to do something. Discretionary performance is happening when we perform above-and-beyond, "at our own discretion." It's the difference between *compliance* (do it only because we have to) and *commitment* (do it because we really want to).

When you unlock behavior, you'll be a delighted witness to daily acts of discretionary performance. You will have tapped into the deepest center of humans that leads them to *want to* do things, without any apparent incentive or motivation.

Developing discretionary performance in employees is especially critical today. The unquestioning loyalty of past generations has all but vanished. Today's workforce seeks engaging work environments that are reciprocal and mutually respectful. Unlocking behavior and tapping into the discretionary performance of all employees is Job One for leaders who want their organizations to win.

A simple fact is that discretionary performance will occur only when the right behaviors are encouraged and people actually become "winners" because those behaviors lead to winning results. The following figure illustrates the three types of leadership and the impact each type has upon performance:

- *Effective leadership, which earns discretionary performance.* This top curve is the one we all want: outstanding discretionary performance, where people perform at peak levels for sustained periods. This is the result of effective leadership that truly "unlocks" employee behavior.

- *Coercive leadership ("do it because I said so"), which earns minimal performance.* This leadership style may get improved performance in the short term, but ultimately creates a work place of fear-driven compliance. People do just enough to get by. Either their performance is just acceptable enough to avoid getting fired, or they carefully achieve the goals set by leaders, but never go beyond. Either way, coercive leadership cannot propel the organization to greatness.

- *Poor leadership, which earns unsatisfactory performance.* Eventually, the unsatisfactory performance comes visible to all stakeholders, and the leader exits or the organization collapses.

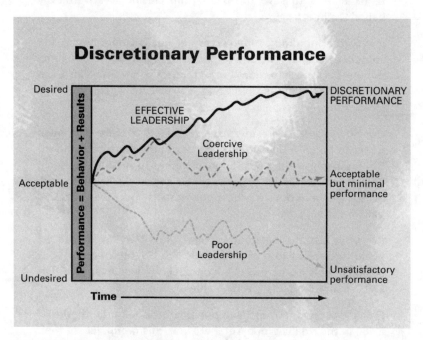

Effective leadership, superior execution, and engaging work environments all depend on your leadership words and actions. *Your behavior—everything you do and say—is the key to tapping **discretionary performance** in yourself and your people.*

CASE EXAMPLE—HOW FOCUSING ON BEHAVIOR MADE THE DIFFERENCE

Here is a memorable experience retold by one of our clients, Brian, who retired as President of a major oil company when it was acquired by a larger peer enterprise. Brian explains how some workers unintentionally taught him a great lesson in leadership: about the impact that his leadership behavior has on results, and about tapping into the discretionary performance of his people.

An experience changed my life some years ago. I ran a refinery in England. Times were tough, and the entire management team labored to save the plant from closing. We frantically bailed the boat.

It was the hundredth anniversary of our UK operations, and someone decided we should celebrate. Our Board provided money for a celebration for a thousand people—£30 each (roughly USD$60)—so we had £30,000 to spend on this celebration.

Honestly, I was more interested in whether there was even going to be an organization next week, than in a celebration! So, I delegated the celebration planning to a small group of blue-collar workers. I gave them the £30,000 and said, "Organize something—have a good time." And I went back to bailing the ship.

So what did the celebration team do? They organized an event equivalent to a county fair in the United States! About 50,000 people came. It was beyond belief! They leveraged that £30,000 and probably got the value of about £1,000,000.

Frankly, we would not have put this little team in charge of £2.50 in their daily work. Yet, here was this group, left to their own devices without any interference or direction from management, and they ran this magnificent event. I mean, it was just incredible!

So my management team and I analyzed this experience to understand how these people had accomplished this tremendous task. It was obvious that they succeeded more than we thought possible, because they were able to exercise their full capabilities. At work we had boxes and barriers all around them.

Ever since this experience, I've been trying to figure how I can tap people's capabilities like that. Why was this team so successful?

- They succeeded because they owned the project, including the consequences of their decisions.
- They had encouraging feedback from their peers, who would evaluate their success using criteria they all understood. (You only celebrate a hundredth anniversary once, and their friends and their families were going to be very rough on them if the event had fallen short!)
- I unwittingly encouraged their behaviors, by simply getting out of their way. I was too busy to deliver any discouraging consequences, intended or unintended! I am positive that if I'd had more time, I would have told them that their plans were unrealistic!

This team had put forth great *discretionary performance*—the effort people *want* to contribute above and beyond what is normally required to keep their jobs.

So: if we always were to manage this way, would it encourage people's continuing discretionary performance? If I were to ensure that employees saw the direct link between their efforts and what they could achieve, then either got out of the way or encouraged them, would it lead to more discretionary performance?

I believe the answer is unequivocally "yes." That's why I'm a leader committed to creating the conditions that encourage these behaviors! It's not always easy, because I have lots of old behaviors that I need to change myself. But I am committed to getting there—for the success of my organization, my people, and myself.

Takeaways from Brian's Story . . .

1. People often have capabilities that are buried or hidden on the job. Our job as leaders is to encourage them—and to create an environment where their capabilities are brought out.

2. The work environment is primarily defined by management, and maintained by the encouraging/discouraging

consequences that people experience. Oftentimes, this work environment unintentionally inhibits discretionary performance and "locks in" minimally acceptable performance.

3. Brian's management instructions ("organize something—have a good time") were very general, compared to the highly specific consequences to the employees of success or failure (expectations of their peers, family members, and community members, Brian's evaluation of their performance, etc.). This demonstrates the power of specific consequences.

4. Brian could have been an even more effective leader if he had pinpointed the behaviors needed for success and created encouraging/desirable consequences. In this story, he did neither, so it's doubtful his people felt like they were "led" by Brian in any meaningful way as they pulled together the event.

5. The Bottom Line: You can unlock behavior and unleash profits in your organization by creating an environment that supports the right behaviors and removes barriers to discretionary performance.

TAKEAWAYS FROM THIS BOOK

We are quite serious when we say that what you read in this book can change not only your leadership but your life. Here are four "behavior facts" that are crucial to every leader's success:

1. *Your behavior—and everyone's—is a response to the environment you work in.* As a leader, you respond to what the corporate environment tells you to do. Your people respond exactly the same way. A truism is that "every organization is perfectly designed right now to produce the results it is getting right now." If you like these results, then you don't need to change the environment. But if you don't like these results, you must change the environment—and you have the power to do so as the leader!

2. *Your leadership behavior profoundly and directly affects everyone within your organization.* You directly influence the environment of the many people below you. You do

this primarily through your direct leadership behavior—what people experience from you daily.

Executives in particular—but all leaders to some degree—often underestimate the impact upon others of what they *do* and *say* (and of what they *don't* do and say). People *watch* and *listen* to leaders very closely—every word and nuance. Leaders need to be mindful of the behavior they demonstrate—and the impact it has on everyone. You also influence how corporate policies, procedures, recognition systems, etc. are used.

In short—you establish and drive your own "corporate culture," which either locks or unlocks behavior (more on corporate culture in Chapter 7).

3. *Leaders have both an economic and moral imperative to unlock behavior in their organizations.* The economic imperative: companies that excel at managing people—at engaging their workforce—far outperform competitors. The moral imperative: people *want* to be engaged in what they do—countless surveys prove this. People contribute more and enjoy work more if their gifts are recognized, leveraged, and appreciated. Leading well and engaging people's hearts and minds really matters—and leading well can be learned, practiced, and mastered.

4. *Powerful behavioral tools are at your fingertips for improving your own leadership behavior and unlocking everyone's performance.* If you heard there was a proven approach for retaining high-potential employees, wouldn't you want to know it? What about a proven way to improve manufacturing cycle time by 70%, or ways to improve customer satisfaction by 25%, or reduce unplanned shutdowns by 40%—wouldn't you want to learn how? How about specific behaviors you can do that would result in your being a markedly better parent, spouse, and friend? Wouldn't you want to know about them?

These are not idle claims. What you will learn from this book is based on decades of research and successful deployment in major corporations—all fully documented.

Ultimately, it all comes down to behavior. As a leader, using these proven behavioral tools, you can create the right work environment—one that engages people's hearts and minds. Further, you will personally enjoy becoming an even better leader whose organization consistently creates superior results.

The IMPACT™ MODEL

Our company has worked to capture our learnings about behavior into a simple, memorable tool that people can easily use wherever they are. The result is the IMPACT™ MODEL—our process for how leaders align and manage critical behaviors. This is the model you can call upon whenever you face a situation where you need individual behavioral change.

This book has been organized around the IMPACT MODEL. In the chapters ahead, we will lead you through a demonstration of just how and why this model works.

Its four steps are purposefully easy: **Identify & Measure** your target results, **Pinpoint** the critical few behaviors needed, **Activate & Consequate** those behaviors, and **Transfer** fluency to sustain the behaviors.

In chapters 2–6, we step through the IMPACT MODEL. After reading these chapters, you'll be able to use the IMPACT MODEL yourself—skillfully. You will be able to determine the behaviors you want in your organization that will consistently produce desired results. You will know how to arrange the work environment to encourage those behaviors up and down the organization. And you will know how to change your own leadership behaviors

IMPACT™ Model

Identify & **M**easure

Target Results

Pinpoint

Critical Few Behaviors

Activate & **C**onsequate

Desired Behavior

Transfer

Fluency to Sustain Behavior

to make things happen while engaging people's hearts and minds.

We hope that you will augment your existing leadership skill set with these incredibly powerful behavioral tools, and reap the rewards we have seen so many other leaders come to enjoy.

On a larger scale, we've used these same basic tools to change how organizations behave—organizations of 350,000 or 35,000 or 3,500 or 350. We've learned that this larger organization change task requires something beyond the **IMPACT MODEL**, so our companion **MAKE-IT™ MODEL** addresses challenges of organization-wide behavior change. Chapter 7 presents this model. You will see that the **MAKE-IT MODEL** for organization behavior change has at its core the **IMPACT MODEL** for individual behavior change.

In Chapter 8, we will visit the oft-overlooked issue of sustainability and transfer of new skills/capabilities to your company's culture. It is not enough to get the behavioral changes rolling; we must ensure they are sustained for the long haul.

Applying Your New Skills

Finally, in Chapter 9, I will show how these new skills can help you with a range of common and important leadership challenges, including:

- Achieving sustained/predictable top-line growth
- Improving customer loyalty, retention, growth
- Boosting innovation across your organization
- Effectively and rapidly integrating cultures and organizations following mergers/acquisitions
- Excelling at executing your strategies
- Boosting employee engagement/retention
- Smoothing leadership transitions and accelerating the new leader and team to hit full stride
- Ensuring that strategic talent management truly results in well-developed leaders

Embedded in each of these topics is the consistent challenge— *to get different results, you must behave differently.*

The science of behavior can be learned by everyone in your organization, thus creating a common framework to quickly figure out how to engage people and get discretionary effort. The behavioral tools and the IMPACT MODEL can be learned and applied by all levels and all functions within your organization.

CASE EXAMPLES THROUGHOUT THIS BOOK

Throughout this book are case examples and success stories from our clients—some of the most-respected leaders and companies in their industries. We include them to illustrate how these companies and leaders have personally demonstrated that these behavioral tools work. Their stories show how they have used these tools and the success they've generated. Some are genuinely inspiring, because they portray how leaders used these behavioral tools to vanquish seemingly unconquerable challenges.

Whether you lead a corporation, a small business, a school, a community group or a Little League team, you will see yourself in these examples, and discover how to be more effective in everything you do and say.

A WORD OF ENCOURAGEMENT . . .

Successful leaders may well see aspects of themselves in this book and say, "This is what I've been doing for most of my career! I just never had it laid out so clearly." If you are one of these people, congratulations! You already know that what you do and say makes all the difference in unlocking people's behavior. Please keep doing it! The world needs more leaders like you. Pass your "book of wisdom" on to others, so they can quickly learn the lessons that you carry so naturally in your head—so they don't have to learn by trial and error.

For newcomers, this can be an eye-opening, even startling, journey. You may end up looking at the world very differently. Many who take this journey become energized to learn new approaches to leading, managing—and perhaps even to conducting their personal relationships and/or how they parent.

If you take these lessons to heart, you will approach issues with new eyes, new understanding, new confidence—and a new degree of effectiveness.

The science herein gives you a framework and a toolset. The analysis gives you insight. The stories give you context, enjoyment, and faith. So, let's begin . . .

Pinpointing the Right Behaviors

"We needed to gain market share to stay competitive. We had strong product reviews and competitive pricing, but sales were flat or slightly down in most territories. Meantime, key competitors were growing 8–14% yearly in the same regions. So I chartered a study team to examine data and analyze root issues. Their conclusion: the problem was our sales teams' performance.

"My study team identified the highest-performing sales reps and recommended that we train the entire sales force in their 'best practices.' So, our sales people had three days of 'best practices' training.

"Three months after the training, we were dismayed to see no real improvements in results. So, we spent more hours observing and interviewing sales reps. Were they using the best practices they had learned? It appeared that most were. Yet, our competition continued to gain market share and our sales stayed flat. Imagine my frustration: I still had not uncovered the key things—behaviors—that we needed to do differently!"

—*VP of Marketing & Sales*
Fortune 500 company

THIS SAD—and common—example has many costs: the negative effects of lost revenues, plus loss of focus, trust, and time with the sales reps. Where this leader failed was in not *selecting the right behaviors for change.*

This VP and his study team didn't know about our **IMPACT MODEL**, yet they had followed its first step: they **Identified** the business need (top line growth in this case) and how to **Measure** the key results they wanted to affect (sales).

Then they assumed they could identify the behaviors of higher-performing sales people, and just train others in those behaviors. Good idea, but they chose the wrong behaviors, ones that did *not* lead to improvement of the targeted measure (sales). They did not understand step two of **IMPACT**, which is **Pinpointing** the critical few behaviors that are really needed.

Pinpointing gives us the framework to identify, analyze, and improve the behavior of every individual involved, from leader to line worker. *And Pinpointing behaviors is the crucial step in linking behavior to results.*

So, once you **Identify** the business opportunity you want to impact and select the targeted results **Measure,** you must **Pinpoint** the *right* behaviors.

GETTING STARTED WITH PINPOINTING

How do you "pinpoint behaviors"? There are two essential steps:

1. Select a critical behavior (or behaviors) from the many that could influence a business result.

2. Describe the behavior (or behaviors) in specific, objective language so it can be communicated, observed, measured, and tracked.

Selection is critical. If you choose a behavior that has no clear connection with business results, you are wasting your time.

How Do You Select a Pinpoint?

"How do I choose the right behaviors to guarantee the results I want?" Here is how—but first a necessary disclaimer: we cannot guarantee you will identify the exact behaviors to positively impact your business. Only you can do that, because of your intimate knowledge of your organization. What we present here is a proven technique.

When we teach pinpointing, we start by asking leaders questions that guide them through the **IMPACT MODEL**. Following is an example—a conversation that our colleague Karen had with her client, Mateo . . .

1st IMPACT Step: <u>IDENTIFY</u>

Karen: Your unit is focusing on improving *x* for the next year because of *y*?

Mateo: Absolutely. That's where the biggest potential lies for gaining a competitive advantage.

Karen: Could you estimate the bottom-line value of that opportunity?

Mateo: Based on *x* and *y*, I believe it's worth *z* to us.

Key points on IDENTIFY—To identify a results target, ask leaders to review their strategy and identify top goals for the year. Then, estimate the bottom-line value for each opportunity. The area with the highest potential return is the best target. Sometimes opportunities of lower dollar value or long-term difficulty in changing are targets, despite other opportunities worth more short-term. The choice can be defined in nonfinancial terms if everyone agrees the potential value is significant. *The business opportunity specified in the initial step of the* **IMPACT MODEL** *should align closely with goals included in written plans or strategy documents.*

2nd IMPACT Step: <u>MEASURE</u>

Karen: Great. To move forward, we need to agree on results measures, so you can align people on the goal and then track their progress.

Mateo: I'd like to use our existing structure for tracking results—our balanced scorecard.

Karen: I agree. Let's look at using the scorecard to (1) clearly identify a results target, (2) communicate that target to affected employees, (3) monitor progress toward the target over time, and (4) organize recognition of achieving the target.

Mateo: OK, here's how the system currently works . . .

Key Points on MEASURE—Many companies already use balanced scorecards, making it easy to measure change in business results. If not, develop measures for the opportunity that are agreed to by key leaders. At a minimum, define current and desired performance to reveal the size of the gap to be closed. Then request a regular reporting process to communicate the status on closing the gap (usually monthly). Regular reporting makes feedback on progress possible.

3rd IMPACT Step: <u>PINPOINT</u>

Pinpoint

Critical Few
Behaviors

Karen: Now let's pinpoint the critical behaviors that contribute to your results target. This means selecting the right behaviors, identifying who performs them, and precisely defining them. Others know more about these behaviors, so we'll need their help. But let's talk it through and consider engaging others to help.

Mateo: OK.

Karen: Could you brainstorm a list of the most critical behaviors and their performers who contribute to the target?

Mateo: Sure. (generates list)

Karen: Wow! If we used the entire list, you and your staff could not manage so many behaviors. So narrow the list; think about one behavior—maybe two—that will have the greatest impact.

Mateo: I can see why I need to include others in this. They probably can do it more effectively. But I think the most important behavior is x.

Karen: Great! You've selected the behavior. Next, define it. You must be very objective so people will clearly understand what it is and how to recognize it. Let's use a tool called the **NORMS OF OBJECTIVITY™**.

Key Points on PINPOINT—

1. Select the Right Behaviors. Guide the leaders in selecting just one or two behaviors that have the greatest impact on results. Ask leaders who know the business to review the lists, choose the person(s) whose behavior has the greatest effect, and identify one to three specific behaviors that would make a difference.

The fewer the pinpoints, the better. Quality-check this step by asking, "If this behavior changed, would you see a significant change in the business results?" If not, return to the drawing board. Select the behavior that if not done well would crash the plane vs. lose the luggage.

2. Describe the Behaviors. Once pinpointed behaviors are chosen, ask leaders to define them using the **NORMS OF OBJECTIVITY,** described in the next section. (Note that we have not yet talked about aligning behaviors that drive results. We'll return to this once you are more familiar with pinpointing.)

A Quick Example of Selecting a Pinpoint

A good example of behavior selection comes from our work with leaders in an operating company that distributes industrial lubricants.

> **The Financial Manager of a key business unit was asked to cut expenses to improve profitability. Prices were already low. Competitors were cutting costs. New, smaller competitors were entering the market. Expense reduction meant survival.**
>
> **"Monthly expenses as a percentage of plan" was identified as the measure. A goal of 95% of planned expenses was set, and management checked measures monthly. A group of managers met with the financial manager to select pinpoints. Rather than identifying specific actions to be taken across the board, they identified a preferred behavior pattern for all managers. Here is how they worded the pinpoint:**
>
> *Meet with direct reports monthly, review expenditures, and identify lines on the budget where reductions can be made. Obtain a commitment from an owner who will take accountability for each reduction. Describe steps necessary to achieve the reduction within a 30-day period.*

In this case, the behaviors involved following a standardized process. The process was repeated each month, but involved no specific budget category or action other than ongoing analysis and selection of budget targets. This approach avoided micromanagement such as "identify and implement steps to decrease travel expenses by 10% across the board," or "negotiate with vendors for a 5% reduction in rates for contract services."

USING "NORMS" TO DESCRIBE A PINPOINTED BEHAVIOR

Pinpointing involves *selecting* a behavior and *describing* it. You have seen how to select behaviors, so let's look at a way to describe them as *objectively* as possible.

We use the **NORMS OF OBJECTIVITY**™ as our test to ensure that we are focusing on *fact*, not interpretations, opinions, or hunches.

For a pinpointed behavior to be described well, it must meet *all five* NORMS criteria: it must Not be an interpretation, must be directly Observable, must be Reliable, must be Measurable, and must be Specific.

This example shows the value of NORMS:

NORMS of Objectivity™

Not an Interpretation

Observable

Reliable

Measurable

Specific

> On one project, I worked with regional sales managers who supervised field reps. The reps were responsible for implementing the company's credit policy, which directly affected receivables and bad debts from nonpaying customers. When I asked the sales managers to pinpoint a critical behavior—a key behavior linked to business results—they selected "respect the credit policies."

Bad choice! That is very subjective, unmeasurable, unspecific. "Respect" is open to interpretation—everyone has a different idea of what "respect" means. If you were asked to "respect the credit policies," would you know what to do? Would you do the same things as someone else? Maybe, maybe not.

This is the tricky part of describing a behavior objectively. Minimize the chance that people will interpret the behavior differently. So . . .

> . . . we asked the sales managers to apply NORMS to make the requirements clearer. Here is what they came up with:
>
> - *Demonstrate understanding of the credit policy by passing an exam at 80% mastery (specific, measurable).*
> - *Inform each customer in writing of the credit terms included in the policies and document this after first meeting with customer (observable, measurable).*
> - *Implement the credit policy by applying penalties for late payment and refusing to sell products to nonpaying customers (observable, measurable).*

This conversion sharply improved the pinpoint by moving from a vague, subjective description to one with observable actions and specific steps. As a result, reps will likely know exactly what to do, and managers will likely know whether the right things are being done.

Each step of NORMS is interesting, and learning this simple tool will change forever how you observe people . . . .

Norms—Not an Interpretation

You immediately get into trouble by describing behaviors in a way that reflects your personal biases, opinions, hunches, or feelings, rather than clear-eyed, dispassionate observation. Interpretations are conclusions or assumptions based in fact, but they express your view instead. Thus they are subjective, not objective. What is needed is honest, careful observation—what you truly see and hear.

Careless or vague behavior descriptions are just as risky, using unspecific words that are wide open to interpretation.

In our sales example, the pinpoint initially proposed was "respect the credit policy." What does "respect" mean? *Carry the policy in your briefcase so you can recite it upon need? Follow it unless there is a good reason to deviate? Document execution of all parts of the policy?* When interpretations like this occur, it usually means that the pinpointed behavior was not stated objectively.

Here are pairs of descriptions. On the left, unspecific wording that is open to interpretation. On the right, an objective version:

Open to Interpretation	Objective Pinpoints
Selling Products	Achieving $5,000 sales/day
(To what standard or level?)	Describing product features to customers
	Sending samples to prospects
Being a team player	Verbally supporting other team members with praise and suggestions
(What does that mean?)	
	Volunteering for team projects
	Completing assigned tasks on time and under budget
Taking unnecessary risks	Refusing to wear safety equipment
(Such as?)	Exceeding parking lot speed limit
	Spending twice the allotted budget on developing a new product line

N☐RMS — ☐bservable

Behavior must be *directly observable*. That is just what it sounds like: action you can observe directly through your senses. Behavior is observable if you can see, hear, touch, taste, or smell it.

Non-observable behavior cannot be sensed directly, and is interpretive, like a "bad attitude," value, or belief. Compare:

Nonobservable Behavior	Observable Behavior
Being a micromanager *(What have you observed to prove this?)*	During review meetings, asking for a root-cause analysis for each instance where performance fell short
Being a model employee *(What have you observed to prove this?)*	Offers to assist other coworkers without prompting Completes assigned tasks on or before due date

Stick to behaviors you can directly *observe*. This is trickier than it sounds. Here is a way: think of yourself as a video camera. Whatever the camera lens sees or whatever the microphone records is true behavior. If you think your boss hates you, ask yourself: "Would a video camera record hatred?" (Of course not. The video might show her frowning or pounding her fist, but that doesn't prove hatred. She could be angry over something completely unrelated to you.)

Try practicing your observation skills the next time you are in a restaurant. Observe people at other tables. Are they happy? Angry? Sad? Preoccupied? Hungry? You can't really tell, because none of that is observable. All you can observe objectively is that they are smiling, laughing, frowning, eating, looking away from the person sitting across from them, etc.

Leaders can directly observe employees' behavior by sampling their performance. For example, "arrives at meetings on time" is observable and a sample of behavior. "Showing commitment to the team" is vague and just a general impression and not a sample. Direct sampling of performance establishes strong points for feedback and measurement.

Observable behaviors are valuable in training, for they can be communicated clearly to people as models for performing well.

NORMS — Reliable

In NORMS, Reliability means that *two or more people agree that they observed the same behavior.* This is a very good test of objectivity. If a pinpointed behavior is subjective, two different observers probably won't agree on what happened.

Think back to the example of the regional sales managers. They defined a critical behavior as "respecting the credit policies." It's unlikely that two people could watch a sales rep and agree on when the rep "respected the credit policy" or didn't.

Here is a classic example, that you may have experienced yourself, of unreliable observation . . .

A VP asked one of his marketing staff to improve her presentations to the marketing team. He called her past presentations "boring" and "too technical." The VP asked her to make the presentations more appropriate for her audience and more lively and interesting. Not knowing NORMS at that time, she accepted these false "pinpoints" and gave it a shot.

During the next meeting, the VP asked two marketing team members to provide feedback. After her performance, the VP, presenter, and two observers met to debrief. One observer said, "You were better than the last time, and the stuff fit well with marketers. But I still feel you need to make some improvements to fit our culture." The other observer told her, "I thought you did a great job. This is a great improvement over your past presentations."

At the end of the debrief, the presenter turned to the VP and said, "Now what?" Clearly there was a *lack of reliability* between the two observers' feedback.

The original behavior pinpoints were poorly defined and led to unreliable observations. The feedback was subjective and general. And the two team members disagreed. Effective behavior change is unlikely to emerge from this situation. So . . .

. . . we suggested they first define what they wanted her to do in factual terms, and then provide feedback on whether or not she showed the pinpointed behaviors. They agreed and settled on the following . . . .

- *Open the presentation with a description of what you will cover . . . spend no more than three minutes.*
- *Then, describe the new product being rolled out. Include the defining features, specs, and how it's different . . . spend about ten minutes.*
- *Smile and maintain eye contact with the audience.*
- *Close your presentation by restating how this new product will benefit the users, including naming the specific problems and complaints it will eliminate.*

NORMS—Measurable

An objective description of behavior must include a way to *measure* it. Examples:

- Byron held face-to-face communication sessions *at all twelve locations within 48 hours* following the merger announcement.
- Francis completed *all six* of the required checks on the equipment.

We need statements that include measurement so we can assess the progress we are making (or lack of it). Here are examples of how specifying *measurable* behavior helps us stay objective:

Not Measurable	Measurable
Our market share in roll-aboard suitcases has really improved. *(This lack of specificity could lead unintentionally to degraded performance. By stating the number more specifically, individuals can monitor performance and make decisions accordingly.)*	Our market share in roll-aboard suitcases has gone from 58% to 71% for three quarters running because: • We've increased the frequency of new customer contacts from 15/month to 25/month. *(The behavior? Contacting new customers)* • We've obtained new distributorships in 20 of 26 strategically targeted cities by offering long-term agreements. *(The behavior? Offering long-term agreements to distributors in strategically targeted cities)*

Not Measurable	Measurable
We are lousy at new product development. *(Without a numerical gauge, individuals have been troubleshooting to improve performance. When behaviors are pinpointed in measurable terms, they can be monitored and managed more carefully and precisely.)*	• New patents filed decreased from 14 to 9 in the last quarter. *(The behavior? Filing patents)* • Submission of new product ideas decreased from 8 to 2. *(The behavior? Submitting new product ideas)*

NORMS — **S**pecific

Finally, the more specific a description is, the better it communicates. Describe your behavioral pinpoints by including who, what, when, where, how, how many, and so on. For example:

General Behavior	Specific Behavior
Juan meets deadlines. *(How can you tell?)*	Juan submitted all required monthly reports prior to the deadline.
Tonya supports her direct reports. *(How can you tell?)*	Tonya meets with her direct reports twice a year to review performance and identify their succession plans.
Mark does sloppy work. *(How can you tell?)*	Mark's past three proposals had several numerical errors in the budget section.

The Goal of NORMS

The goal is not just to make pinpoints objective. *The goal is to establish a pinpoint that can be communicated to people so they understand exactly what to do and how to recognize when they do it.* Be as objective as necessary to accomplish this goal. In other words, be as NORMS-based as necessary to establish common understanding of the behavior.

But don't go overboard in being specific. It would be silly to tell a direct report, "I want you to contribute four comments, each between 30 and 90 seconds in length, in every meeting we have." Reasonable specificity would be, "I want you to make one or two constructive suggestions in our next meeting." The latter statement is enough to establish a common understanding of the desired behavior.

Quick Recap

Remember where we started: It is critical to **Identify** your business opportunity and the results **Measures** you wish to achieve. Then, **Pinpoint** the behaviors you need to meet the objective.

*Selecting clear **Pinpoints** and defining them objectively* prepares you for the third step in the **IMPACT MODEL**. That step, **Activate & Consequate**, helps you to increase the influence of the pinpointed behaviors toward your desired results.

GETTING THE PINPOINT RIGHT

To illustrate, here's a story that starts with getting the pinpoint *wrong:*

> Global Telecom launched a major sales initiative to upsell services. Their Customer Service Representatives (CSRs) frequently talked with clients, so the company decided to have them do upselling of enhanced services when customers called for help. The company spent heavy time and resources on training CSRs to sell new packages. They also provided strong incentives for selling.
>
> How well did it work? Well, the CSRs had always seen themselves in a "helping" role. So, they were deeply offended by being asked to sell. In fact, the company had a near-rebellion, with the threat of union grievances. Neither sales nor customer service ratings improved—nor did morale.

And here is how they regrouped and got the pinpoint *right:*

> Then the company looked hard at the behaviors needed to achieve the business result of upselling . . . .

> Global Telecom refocused its efforts. Instead of pushing "selling," they promoted "needs-based solutions." CSRs were trained in uncovering customers' needs and creating the best match between a customer's needs and the company's services.

> Training consisted of learning the services and developing good customer service skills: active listening, questioning, speaking, selecting opportunities, etc. Training also provided feedback, coaching, and recognition for performing the right behaviors.

> In fact, to further strengthen their commitment to the sales system, the CSRs were actually encouraged to downsell if it better met the customers' needs! Because downselling had always been such a taboo, CSRs were leery of doing it. In fact, early in the program, the managers and coaches actually held daily end-of-shift events to celebrate downselling!

> This time, the CSRs were delighted with their new role. After all, they were now meeting customers' needs—helping them—better than ever. And sales increased 35%.

Of course sales increased! This time, the company pinpointed the right behaviors, and managed them right. Rather than focusing on selling strategies, the company focused on the behaviors that CSRs needed to better understand and meet the needs of customers.

KEEP BEHAVIORAL PINPOINTING STRATEGICALLY FOCUSED

Dr. Bill Redmon, a close colleague and friend, offers a favorite example of behavioral pinpointing. It demonstrates the need for a relentless pursuit of strategically important pinpointed behaviors . . . .

> Bill was coaching a Vice President and his team of General Managers. Each GM was responsible for a strategic business

unit, including P&L, new product development, technology, and marketing/sales. The GMs felt they already were helping immediate profits by managing spending, and affecting long-term success by hitting milestones for development projects.

During pinpointing discussions, each GM agreed that *new product development* was the most challenging area, because the process was difficult to understand and manage. Clearly, they felt this to be a significant business opportunity.

So Bill asked how they would *measure success.* None wanted to use day-to-day details. Instead, they wanted to track the impact on business: (1) *track expenditures as a percentage of budget* and (2) *track percentage of project milestones achieved monthly and year-to-date.*

Bill had them identify performers who affected these results and list their behaviors that linked to results. The GMs identified the Project Managers as most influential and listed these behaviors:

- *Hold weekly team meetings to review expenditures and provide feedback*
- *Review only purchases above $5,000 to ensure the most efficient purchasing procedures are used, and provide feedback to Purchasing Agents*
- *Identify milestones at risk and take action early*
- *Arrange for external quality reviews and follow up within 10 days on out-of-compliance items*

Then Bill had them pick *the single behavior that would make the greatest difference in staying within budget and on schedule.* They rank-ordered and identified *"Hold weekly team meetings to review expenditures and provide feedback"* as the highest-leverage behavior. Some also highly ranked *"Identify milestones at risk and take action early."* They elected to focus on both pinpoints.

This completed the selection part of pinpointing. They knew who the performers were and what behaviors they needed to manage. They also selected behaviors that were powerful drivers for the results they needed.

Bill then had the team carefully define the pinpointed behaviors so all project teams would understand what they

needed to do. This also allowed GMs to measure progress easily. Here is their description:

Meet with the entire project team each Friday morning. Review the weekly reports of expenditures against budget for each major category. Review milestones achieved, at risk, and missed. For each item over-budget or off-schedule, develop a specific plan to correct the deviation. Identify an owner for the plan and a due date for each major step.

As a project team member: Wouldn't you like to have that clear description of desired behavior? It truly clarifies what is expected. And it gives you a way to recognize when you are on target, because it is NORMS-based.

As a leader: Wouldn't you like to have that clear description of desired project team behavior? It establishes your expectations for the project team and gives you a way to recognize when the team is on target. Further, when you see team members engaging in the pinpointed behavior, you have a clear opportunity to provide positive feedback.

> **CAUTION! (Just One Or Two Behaviors, Please)**
>
> It is tempting to select many pinpointed behaviors, but this is a trap! You only need to focus on one or two critical behaviors to make the biggest difference. The key is selecting the right ones.
>
> Analyzing and managing behaviors takes time and energy. If too many behaviors are pinpointed, leaders end up overloaded, because they must consistently manage each behavior. This extra workload can dampen the enthusiasm of even the most dedicated leader.

The bottom line: *pinpointing behaviors you want allows you to be a proactive leader.* It helps you proactively create business results by managing behaviors that drive those results.

THE BIGGER PICTURE: ALIGN ALL PINPOINTS TO MAXIMIZE RESULTS

Another key aspect of pinpointing is *alignment of key behaviors to impact results*. Different departments can identify their own pinpoints, but it is important to organize multiple pinpoints to create an overall, coordinated impact on business results. Business results occur best when behavior is aligned across all performers or work units. If one group's behavioral pinpoints are not aligned with others, you will be missing a piece of the puzzle.

Here's an example that shows how behavioral pinpoints can be organized across multiple units to quickly produce significant results.

Identify the Business Opportunity . . .

Tough times at *PCs by the Ton,* a computer sales/distribution company. Order errors, inaccurate invoicing, late deliveries, and damaged shipments brought a monsoon of customer complaints and loss of market share in this fiercely competitive industry. *PCs by the Ton* saw their biggest opportunity: improving end-to-end processing of customer orders.

. . . and the Results Measure . . .

Managers created the Exact Order Index (EOI) to track effectiveness in end-to-end order processing. The EOI included effectiveness measures at key points in the process. It generated a total score from 0 (under half of customer specs met) to 10 (perfect performance). The target was 9; average EOI at project start was 6. Managers calculated that an average score of 9 would ensure 98% of the customers were completely satisfied.

. . . then Pinpoint and Align Behaviors That Drive Results

Key jobs for the end-to-end process were identified in four work units—Order Input, Assembly & Testing, Invoicing, and Shipping. Behaviors related to target results were pinpointed for each key job in each work unit. Here is a sample:

Work Unit	Pinpointed Behaviors
Order Input	• Within 4 hours of phone or fax order, create complete customer order form • Input order information without error • Forward completed order to Assembly & Testing
Assembly & Testing	• Obtain units identified on product order form • Insert components into right box with packing materials & latest manual for each component
Invoicing	• Enter materials codes and unit prices • Calculate total price and ensure that credit card transfer of payment is approved • Forward final invoice with equipment & manuals in sealed container with complete customer address to Shipping
Shipping	• Complete shipping label & arrange for pickup • Track package to final delivery & confirm receipt in perfect condition • Resolve shipping problems to customer's satisfaction within 24 hours of detection

The end-to-end process required coordinated behaviors from several people in key jobs. The pinpoints defined the behaviors needed for successful Exact Orders. All behaviors across the units needed to be organized and managed together. As a group with shared accountability for the entire process, the managers pinpointed behaviors and set up a plan for managing each behavior to create a high EOI score.

Any compromise at a key point in the process undermined the entire process and created customer dissatisfaction. So, pinpoints had to be organized across work groups, requiring a cross-functional effort. To ensure this, all managers agreed to pinpoint and manage key behaviors during the same timeframe.

MEASURING BEHAVIOR

Most leaders are very good at measuring results—operating margins, sales, etc. Few track behaviors in the same way, but it's important to do so—it allows you to be more aware of what is happening at the individual and work-group levels.

Good measurement helps you see how to change behaviors when you don't get the results you expect. Measurement also helps you identify successes to celebrate and problems to attack. Finally—perhaps most valuably—good measurement helps you observe and track important pinpoints so you can learn more about behavior and whether it is working for you or against you.

Measurement adds incredible power to your leadership tool set.

How Come We Don't Measure Very Often?

Determining *what to measure* and *how*, and whether to measure both behaviors and results or mainly one or the other, can get pretty detailed. This explains why companies generally are weak at measuring behaviors. First, it's hard to do, and can take a lot of time—behavioral pinpointing is hard work. Second, we all have experienced measures that produced too much data and too little information. Don't lose sight of the purpose: *to collect data for evaluating success and guiding analysis and action.*

In our experience, simpler measures work best. A few checkmarks in a notebook beats an automated spreadsheet *if* the notebook measures are collected consistently for important behaviors that can be altered to improve the business.

We view behavior as only a cost until its value is clearly defined and its return on investment can be determined. After all, behavior spent on one initiative is diverted from another. Behavior spent in the classroom or coaching sessions is behavior not invested in sales, manufacturing, shipping, or project management. We suggest that you view behavior like a stock purchase—an investment of known quantity (time and effort) in an area that is very likely to deliver a profit (return on investment).

TAKEAWAYS ON PINPOINTING

Here are your key points to take from this chapter:

1. *The IMPACT MODEL helps you apply the science of behavior to create real business results.* The model guides you through aligning behaviors with business results. In the next few chapters, you will learn how to use the model to proactively manage behaviors to create results. (*For more on the MAKE-IT MODEL, please visit www.clg.com.*)

2. *Always start by Identifying the business opportunity and concrete results measures.*

3. *Results Measures are always the foundation for behavioral targets (Pinpoints).* Developing a pinpoint involves two steps:

    - *Select the right behavior*—identify the many behaviors that contribute to results and then select the one or two top contributors. The fewer the pinpoints, the better. Quality-check this step by asking, "If this behavior changed, would you see a significant change in the business results?" If not, return to the drawing board. Select the behavior that if not done well would crash the plane vs. lose the luggage.

    - *Describe the behavior*—use the NORMS OF OBJECTIVITY to precisely describe the desired behavior.

    The NORMS OF OBJECTIVITY is your tool for describing behavioral pinpoints objectively.

NORMS of Objectivity™

Not an Interpretation

Observable

Reliable

Measurable

Specific

4. *Pinpointing is not always enough to create success.* You must also ensure that pinpoints are aligned, because people in other departments or levels also influence results. Everyone's behavioral pinpoints must be aligned.

Our next step in the **IMPACT** MODEL is to **Activate & Consequate,** where we proactively manage behavior to create business results. In the next two chapters, we will focus on the foundational pieces of Behavioral Science that pull it all together. Once you master these principles, you will understand what you need to do to manage behavior.

Highlighting Excellence . . .

IMPACT™ MODEL Helps Align 5,300 CIGNA Employees

I n 2006, CIGNA Health Care became the first national health carrier recognized for delivering "An Outstanding Customer Service Experience" in member call center operations by J.D. Power and Associates through their Call Center Certification Program^{SM}.

This is an amazing tribute to any group, but for CIGNA's service employees, it represents a particularly remarkable accomplishment. Just four years prior to receiving the award, the company had implemented a new technology infrastructure, which sometimes impacted service delivery—and frustrated customers, providers, and CIGNA HealthCare employees. This resulted in a claims processing backlog, triggering higher-than-normal call volumes. Morale suffered and turnover increased.

That was the situation inherited by Scott Storrer, when he was handpicked by CIGNA CEO Edward Hanway to lead the CIGNA HealthCare Service Operations. He had to turn things around quickly.

Where did Storrer begin? "We first met with our customers," he recalled. "We asked for their confidence and a bit of patience while we took immediate, decisive steps to reverse the tide."

He did indeed. Over the next six months, Storrer led the rapid implementation of significant process redesign, technology modifications, and new hiring practices. It was an intensive improvement effort—and it worked.

"We'd done a good job of stabilizing and improving the environment," he stated. "But we determined that the new processes didn't always stick—people reverted to their comfort zones."

That's when Storrer met with CLG Senior Partner Steve Jacobs, who suggested that a performance lift might require new and specific behaviors from his team. "It's one thing to define better ways of working, and another to get people using them in the field," Jacobs said.

"In theory, this sounded correct," Storrer said. "But could we achieve the sustained focus needed with 5,300 employees? I was intrigued, but not convinced."

CIGNA HealthCare decided to implement CLG's *Performance Catalyst®* process, using the IMPACT™ Model, across many managers and leaders in two of the company's service centers.

One of the key steps in implementation was to follow the IMPACT Model and pinpoint critical path behaviors—the day-to-day actions that most directly impact desired performance. Gathering front-line employee and supervisor input, the site leadership team and our CLG colleague, Brian Cole, worked in alignment sessions to specify targeted results and pinpoint key behaviors required to drive those results at all levels, from claims processors up to the SVP.

Next, the site management team received Performance-Based Leadership™ (PBL) training, with a focus on establishing consistent skills and approaches for fostering critical path behaviors, creating manager-specific coaching action plans, and practicing through structured rehearsals.

Ongoing coaching, provided by Cole and his team, "was essential to the sustainability of the program," said Storrer. "By aligning results to behaviors, measuring these expected behaviors, and following up with regular coaching, we set the stage for the change to become business as usual."

Feedback up and down the organization also became a regular activity. Employees asked for and received input from their supervisors; supervisors also worked to remove barriers to desired behaviors.

The IMPACT implementations were conducted in the midst of other ongoing improvement initiatives within CIGNA HealthCare. The cumulative effect of those efforts was impressive—so much so that in 2005, CIGNA HealthCare rolled out the IMPACT process to its five other call centers.

Although initially skeptical, Storrer pointed out that pinpointing has aligned 5,300 people on the critical behaviors required to make their service model work.

Surveys indicate a significant increase in customer satisfaction with CIGNA HealthCare's claim and call services, compared to its major competitors. In 2005, CIGNA HealthCare rose impressively among the top-ten insurance providers. The recognition from J.D. Power demonstrates CIGNA HealthCare's commitment to satisfying their call center customers.

For information on J.D. Power and Associates Certified Call Center Program[SM], see www.jdpower.com

Managing Behavior: Know Your ABCs!

"SellMation spent over $6 million implementing this state-of-the-art sales automation system. It was to improve our efficiency by 50–75%.

"Everyone was trained on it—directors, managers, supervisors, and salespeople. But fewer than half of our people are actually using it! And we have not seen the savings promised—in fact, our problems have increased, because we have some folks operating with information from outdated printed reports. Now we have inconsistency in product pricing out there with distributors and customers.

"Implementation has been a disaster. We were better off before this change!"

—*Disgruntled Executive*

H OW OFTEN WE HEAR some version of that executive's story as we work with corporate leaders! Their problems often center on technology initiatives (as in the example above) or culture change, quality, or cross-selling. This is appalling, considering the hundreds of millions spent yearly on initiatives to improve business results!

Too often, there is the big announcement, the flurry of activity, but only a temporary improvement. By now, you know why: *It's because implementation efforts and plans rarely address people's behavior.*

Implementation maps out processes and new interfaces, but most leaders do not apply behavioral knowledge when managing people. This leaves implementation, planning, and behavior unaligned—and leaves them all to chance.

Leaders invest a lot in doing the right things. They "create the compelling vision" and "communicate the vision" so it "links strategy to people." They "involve people" in planning the change. They "align processes with the vision." They "create champions and owners" at all levels of the organization.

This all sounds like a focus on behavior, but it's not. It doesn't address what people really do and say. It may *inspire* change, but inspiration doesn't make change happen. *It takes new behavior or different behavior to make change happen.*

In Chapter 2 you learned about **Pinpointing** behaviors—selecting those that most impact the result you want. In this chapter, we move to the next step in our **IMPACT MODEL:** to **Activate & Consequate** the chosen behaviors.

This is the truly analytical part that appeals to so many leaders we have worked with. This is the ABC analysis, which lets you see clearly why critical behaviors aren't occurring, and how you can get them to— consistently.

UNDERSTANDING BEHAVIOR STARTS WITH THE ABC ANALYSIS

To implement any change, you need to know your ABCs: *Antecedents*, *Behaviors*, and *Consequences*. These three elements are powerfully related:

- Antecedents trigger **Behaviors** (A ➡ B)
- **Behaviors** are followed by **Consequences** (B ⬌ C) that in turn determine whether the behaviors will recur (thus the two-way arrow)

Here is the concept again, in ABC analysis format:

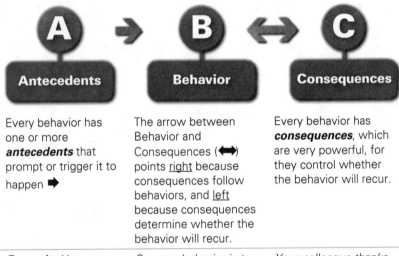

Antecedents	Behavior	Consequences
Every behavior has one or more **antecedents** that prompt or trigger it to happen ➡	The arrow between Behavior and Consequences (⬌) points <u>right</u> because consequences follow behaviors, and <u>left</u> because consequences determine whether the behavior will recur.	Every behavior has **consequences**, which are very powerful, for they control whether the behavior will recur.
Example: You observe a colleague working late and frantically ➡ . . .	*So, your behavior is to stay and help your colleague ⬌ . . .*	*Your colleague thanks you (making you more likely to stay and help again)–or–your colleague doesn't thank you (making it less likely you will stay and help again).*

This concept of ABCs (Antecedents-Behavior-Consequences) gives us a consistent technique for analyzing behaviors—both current ones and the new ones we desire.

> **The ABCs is a snapshot of behavior and its surrounding environment:**
>
> **Antecedents ➡ Behavior ⬌ Consequences**
>
> It is valuable for two reasons:
>
> - To understand why certain behaviors occur, or don't
> - To identify strategies for encouraging desired behaviors and discouraging undesired behaviors

The following figure shows important characteristics of Antecedents, Behaviors, and Consequences:

Antecedents	Behavior	Consequences
• Are events that *precede* or *prompt* behavior	• What a person says or does	• Are events that *follow* behavior
• Have only short-term effects, unless paired with consequences	• Pinpointed behaviors correlate with business results	• Increase, maintain, or decrease behavior
• Have much less impact on behavior than consequences		• Have great influence on whether behavior occurs again
• Are overused compared to consequences		• Positive, encouraging consequences are the most desirable & effective

Examples: *training, vision statements, individual abilities, behavior of others, past events, requests, goal statements, pep talks, safety posters*	***Examples:*** *attend a meeting, place a call, complete a form, record time spent on a project, correct an error*	***Examples:*** *acknowledgment, feedback, bonus, awards, completion of a task, token of appreciation*

THE SELLMATION CASE

Let us return to our opening story about the SellMation executive losing $6 million, and look deeper at the sales automation system that so perplexed him . . .

SellMation developed an impressive technology solution for its salespeople: software that gave them direct access to pricing, inventory, manufacturing schedules, etc. The empowered project team helped select vendors, customize the system, plan implementation, and oversee the rollout across SellMation's regions and divisions.

The objectives were clear: improve data-entry efficiency, improve data accuracy, and cut order response time to distributors and customers. As the team analyzed workflow, they found errors and value-reducing delays during handoffs. So, they had salespeople interface directly with the data, eliminating several handoffs. Fewer keystrokes were required to process an order. At first, everyone seemed very pleased.

Then they discovered one little oversight: the team never really looked at how using the new software would impact the salespeople's *behavior*. As our hapless executive said, "Implementation has been a total failure!"

Here is what the team missed: salespeople had always relied on customer service representatives (CSRs) to enter pricing, enter orders, and gather/track data. The new system did require fewer keystrokes—but under the old system, salespeople didn't key in *anything*. So, to them, elimination of CSRs created a huge increase in what they had to do—a real step backward!

Further, in the old system, a salesperson who needed information simply phoned a CSR—an efficient use of time, using their cell phones between customer visits, plus they enjoyed the social interaction with CSRs. But now they had to lug laptops along, find an Internet connection or signal, and navigate it to get information.

The whole problem was that the new software required dramatic changes in behaviors. And in this implementation, those behaviors were neither acknowledged nor planned for.

Behavior change was the cornerstone of this change imple-mentation.

So the salespeople revolted, refusing to use laptops to get data, regardless of how well the software worked. They didn't want to invest the time or energy in traveling with a laptop and a thick manual and having to log on after a long day. And they dreaded the hassle of connecting from client sites, where Internet access was iffy.

The bottom line: **the time spent fiddling with laptops and entering orders was time lost with customers, when they could have generated more business, earned commissions, and helped achieve the company's stretch goals!**

(For those who relate personally to this story, we will share later in this chapter how we mitigated the negative consequences of the new system!)

The problem here is clear: this new software system required new behaviors from the salespeople, *and the consequences for those behaviors were negative.* The consequences virtually guar-anteed an implementation failure—and there would assuredly be no discretionary performance.

Now, what could this executive (or the original implementa-tion team) do to get the new behaviors going, and go smoothly from their *present* behaviors to the *new* ones needed for the change to happen?

They could *pinpoint critical behaviors of key performers—*salespeople in the field—behaviors that were necessary for this software investment to pay off.

Then, they could create encouraging consequences to make those new behaviors happen. This is where the ABC analysis comes in.

A Critical Behavior: Phoning a CSR

A critical behavior in our example is *phoning a CSR* (to get pricing, place an order, check shipping).

The Antecedents. Why did salespeople, under the old system, call CSRs? Their training manual said to, and they were told to do so by other sales reps. Both reasons are *antecedents*—events that come before a behavior and prompt it to happen. Here is an ABC analysis:

Performer: Salespeople

Antecedents	Behavior	Consequences
• Told by sales reps to call CSRs • Sales manual instructions	Call CSR to place order and check pricing	

Remember that antecedents occur before a behavior, set the stage for it to happen, get it started, and tell people how we want them to behave. So, **Antecedents** triggered the *call-a-CSR* behavior from the salespeople.

The Consequences. And why did the sales reps continue to call CSRs? Because of **Consequences.** They continued the behavior because they received a positive payoff—they got a price or question answered, learned a shipping date, etc.

These are all **Consequences**—events that follow a behavior and affect whether it will recur and how often. *Consequences are directly linked to a behavior in a way that either encourages it to happen again, or discourages it from happening again.*

Here is the same ABC analysis, with consequences added:

Performer: Salespeople

Antecedents	Behavior	Consequences
• Told by sales reps to call CSRs • Sales manual instructions	Calling CSR to place order and check pricing	• Got questions answered • Learned shipping dates • Got pricing • Closed a sale • Got to talk with CSR friends and colleagues

You can see that the consequences for "calling a CSR" continually encourage that behavior. The old way worked well, salespeople liked it—so no wonder they rebelled against the new system and new behaviors required.

It is ironic that in business, where bright people always seek better ways to do things, *consequences are greatly underused as a means of influencing behaviors—especially positive, encouraging consequences.* Once you learn to effectively manage consequences for the behaviors you need in your organization, you will get results.

WHY IS BUSINESS CULTURE SO ANTECEDENT-HEAVY?

Especially in corporate settings, leaders rely on antecedents to foster new behaviors. When that fails, they just pile on more antecedents (get a bigger hammer): issue memos, pep talks, training manuals, and restate expectations. The result? Wonderful initiatives are kicked off, ride high awhile, and then decline, sputter, or go away altogether.

The problem is that these antecedents have only about a 20% influence over what we say or do. Consequences have about 80% influence. (Note to self: use consequences, not antecedents.)

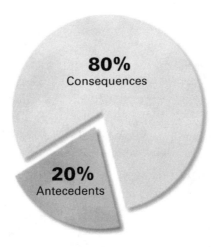

Consequences are much more powerful influencers on behavior than antecedents—and four times more effective!

Think about those training classes on "what it means to be a leader." Those classes are antecedents for desirable leadership behavior. So newly trained leaders emerge from these classes, eager to "be a great leader."

Then they see very different real-world leadership behaviors of people at higher levels. They also see people with totally different leadership styles getting promoted. These observations are powerful consequences that encourage new leaders to behave *opposite of the way they were taught or told.*

So, the antecedents prompt the "talk," but the real consequences dictate the "walk." Leaders whose "talk" and "walk" don't match confuse the very people they are trying to develop as future leaders. Ultimately, consequences prevail—and so do unwanted behaviors.

Personal Note: Consequences at Home

The ABCs really hit home when you try to change your children's behaviors. One executive with two teenage daughters confessed, "I had been using 500 pounds of antecedents and no consequences for most of my parenting lifetime. No wonder I've gone gray fast, and still have teens who do as they please!

"I realized that I've spent most of our interactions demanding they do things I think are important. But those all have been just antecedents. I needed to be providing **positive consequences** for what they were doing right or well . . .

"I was tired of my own voice repeating: 'Why isn't your room clean?' 'Have you finished your homework?' 'You're not going out dressed like that, are you?' 'Set the table before you get on the phone.'

"I realized that my daughters were doing a lot of behaviors I was proud of, but not encouraging. I had missed opportunities to make us all happier.

"But I also learned it is never too late to change! Once I began to say 'Thanks for making your bed—I know you were pressed for time before school,' or 'I appreciate your clearing the table after dinner, especially without your mom or me asking,' I noticed that they did more of those things, and more joyfully. In focusing on consequences more than antecedents, I discovered they really had a lot of desired behaviors to praise and appreciate—and many fewer undesired behaviors to address!"

HOW ANTECEDENTS WORK

Now that you've seen an overview of the ABC analysis, you know that the B part of ABC—the behavior—is the foundation of the analysis. Pinpointing the critical **Behaviors** is always the first step:

Before each behavior come **Antecedents.** Antecedents either set the stage for a behavior (like training), or actually prompt or trigger it to occur (like a ringing phone):

Common antecedents for behavior in the workplace include:

- Training
- Job aids
- Individual skills
- Behaviors of others
- Request to do something
- Vision statements

- Telling people what to do
- Equipment operation
- Performance objectives
- Time of day
- Posters, signs, or banners
- E-mail reminders

Antecedents set up the conditions that make behavior more *likely,* but they do not guarantee its occurrence. For example, a traffic light turning yellow is an antecedent for your behavior of hitting the brake in your car. Seeing a yellow light makes you more likely to stop—but doesn't guarantee you will stop every time—instead, you might run the yellow light.

Here are more examples of **Antecedents (A)** that prompt our **Behavior (B)**, but which may be less apparent:

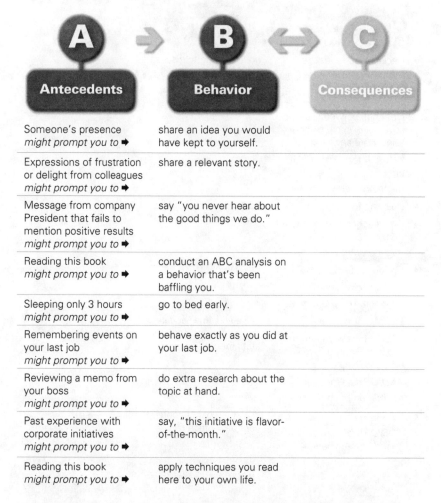

Antecedents	Behavior
Someone's presence *might prompt you to* ➡	share an idea you would have kept to yourself.
Expressions of frustration or delight from colleagues *might prompt you to* ➡	share a relevant story.
Message from company President that fails to mention positive results *might prompt you to* ➡	say "you never hear about the good things we do."
Reading this book *might prompt you to* ➡	conduct an ABC analysis on a behavior that's been baffling you.
Sleeping only 3 hours *might prompt you to* ➡	go to bed early.
Remembering events on your last job *might prompt you to* ➡	behave exactly as you did at your last job.
Reviewing a memo from your boss *might prompt you to* ➡	do extra research about the topic at hand.
Past experience with corporate initiatives *might prompt you to* ➡	say, "this initiative is flavor-of-the-month."
Reading this book *might prompt you to* ➡	apply techniques you read here to your own life.

Multiple Antecedents Can Trigger the Same Behavior

Clearly understanding the **Antecedent-Behavior** relationship is your first step in understanding why **Behaviors** occur. Also, multiple **Antecedents** can combine to trigger **Behaviors**:

Multiple Antecedents Can Trigger the Same Behavior

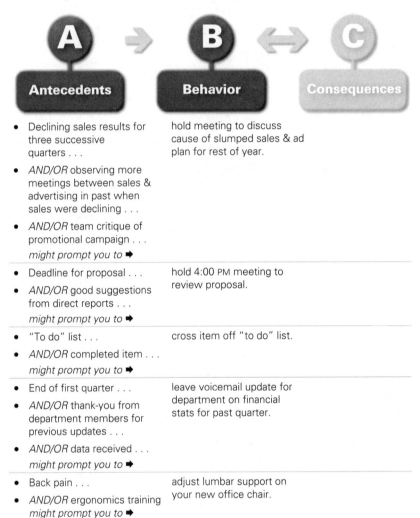

Antecedents	**Behavior**	**Consequences**
• Declining sales results for three successive quarters . . . • *AND/OR* observing more meetings between sales & advertising in past when sales were declining . . . • *AND/OR* team critique of promotional campaign . . . *might prompt you to* ➡	hold meeting to discuss cause of slumped sales & ad plan for rest of year.	
• Deadline for proposal . . . • *AND/OR* good suggestions from direct reports . . . *might prompt you to* ➡	hold 4:00 PM meeting to review proposal.	
• "To do" list . . . • *AND/OR* completed item . . . *might prompt you to* ➡	cross item off "to do" list.	
• End of first quarter . . . • *AND/OR* thank-you from department members for previous updates . . . • *AND/OR* data received . . . *might prompt you to* ➡	leave voicemail update for department on financial stats for past quarter.	
• Back pain . . . • *AND/OR* ergonomics training *might prompt you to* ➡	adjust lumbar support on your new office chair.	

What Are YOUR Antecedents?

Your every behavior, every day, has antecedents. At the simplest level, if the antecedent is thirst, your behavior is to drink some water. But what are your workday behaviors and their antecedents?

What Are YOUR Antecedents?

Think about five behaviors—things you did or said—at work today. Write them in the RIGHT-hand column.

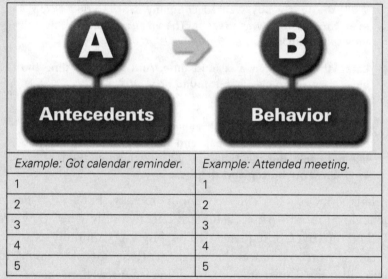

Example: Got calendar reminder.	Example: Attended meeting.
1	1
2	2
3	3
4	4
5	5

Now, to the LEFT of each behavior, write the **antecedent(s)** that prompted each behavior. (Use the example as a model for wording.)

Tips for identifying antecedents:

- First, be sure you have a clearly pinpointed behavior—use the **NORMS OF OBJECTIVITY** as a check.

- To help discover the antecedents of your behaviors, ask yourself these questions:

  - What happens right before the behavior?
  - What triggers the behavior?
  - What cues prompt behavior?

When Antecedents Fail: Crying Wolf

An **Antecedent** can be effective in *starting* a **Behavior**, but it may not last. The fable of the shepherd boy who cried "Wolf!" illustrates this point:

> The boy had the lonely task of tending the village's sheep while they grazed on the mountainside during the day. The community had arranged a signal (*antecedent*): if the boy cried "Wolf!" the village residents would run to protect their sheep (*behavior*).
>
> Well, the lonely boy wanted company. So he cried "Wolf!" even though none was present. The villagers raced to his aid, only to find no wolf.
>
> Later, the boy did it a second time. And a second time the villagers went to his aid, but found no wolf.
>
> Then the boy cried "Wolf!" a third time, because this time there truly *was* a large wolf eyeing up the sheep, licking its chops and circling the sheep and the boy, his eyes glowing like hot coals. But this time, the villagers ignored the cry. The wolf dined on mutton and shepherd boy.

This story teaches children about honesty, but it also has a behavioral moral: **Antecedents** are effective only when they are backed up by **Consequences**. The boy's cry initially was an effective **Antecedent** for the villagers' **Behavior** of running to help. But the **Consequences** of doing so proved negative, repeatedly. Villagers ran to help, only to find that nothing was wrong—they wasted their time and energy on a false alarm, twice.

So, the villagers' **consequence history** became one of "false alarm, don't bother." And so the **Antecedent** became ineffective for initiating the **Behavior**.

Consequence History

Everyone builds a consequence history as a result of their behavior. When you say something like "my experience tells me not to believe that," it is your consequence history talking. The consequences of your past behaviors, or behaviors of others you have seen or been made aware of, have accumulated into a history that guides your future behavior.

> ### Consequence History . . .
>
> A person's cumulative experience of encouraging and discouraging consequences for specific behaviors and/or antecedents. Some like to call it our "memory." Consequence histories establish people's readiness to perform certain behaviors. If your behavior has been discouraged in the presence of certain people or situations, you will be reluctant to engage in that behavior again in the presence of same or similar antecedents.

The same thing happens in organizations. We issue vision statements about fundamentally different ways of operating . . . getting closer to the customer than ever before . . . investing in our people and their development . . . being better at planning and anticipating so we can be proactive rather than reactive . . . .

All of these antecedents are intended to prompt behaviors, such as demonstrating enthusiasm for the vision, revising our work processes to accomplish the company's goals, and working closely with others to improve how we do our jobs.

But when consequences just reinforce the old ways of doing things, or when they are clearly inconsistent with strong change statements, employees end up with the same consequence history as the villagers when they heard "Wolf!"—false alarm, don't bother. Employees say, "The only sign around here we believe is the one that says *WET PAINT.*"

THE "RULE" OF CONSEQUENCES

There is a **Consequence** for *every* behavior—no exceptions.

For example, sending an e-mail is a behavior. Every e-mail you send has some **Consequence** that will affect your future e-mailing behavior. **Consequences** you may receive are an encouraging response, a discouraging response, or no response (just a "mail sent" message). Each of these **Consequences** is encouraging or discouraging to you, and each strongly affects your e-mailing behavior in the future.

Recalling the SellMation salespeople who called customer service reps with orders and questions—what were the **Consequences** for their behavior of calling CSRs? Here is the ABC analysis with consequences:

Performer: Salespeople

A Antecedents	B Behavior	C Consequences
• Told by sales reps to call CSRs • Sales manual instructions	Call CSR to place order and check pricing	• Got questions answered • Learned shipping dates • Got pricing • Got info quickly while doing other things • Got to talk with CSR friends & colleagues

That's quite a few very desirable, encouraging **Consequences.** But then reps were told to *stop* calling CSRs and *start* the new behavior of logging on for information. Undesirable consequences replaced desirable consequences.

> ### Tips for Identifying Consequences
>
> • Make sure you have clearly pinpointed a behavior.
> • Ask yourself:
>   • What does the performer experience as a result of the behavior?
>   • What happens to the performer as a result of the behavior?
>   • What events immediately after the behavior are likely to impact the performer (either encouraging or discouraging)?
>
> Most likely, the answers will be your consequences.

The Power of Consequences

We can't emphasize enough that **Consequences** have the greatest influence on behavior! They either *increase* or *decrease* its occurrence. It is important to understand both possibilities. Here is an example of each . . .

Increasing Behavior. Consider your head of staff, who writes performance evaluations, reviews financials, and ensures that all contractual documents are current. The **Antecedents** for her behavior include (1) her commitment to you to ensure budgets are not exceeded, (2) discounts on legal fees if contracts get renewed before the expiration date, (3) her scheduler reminding of performance discussions with direct reports, and (4) quiet time in the office with the rest of staff absent.

All of these **Antecedents** are *prompting* her behavior, as shown in this ABC analysis:

Performer: Head of Staff

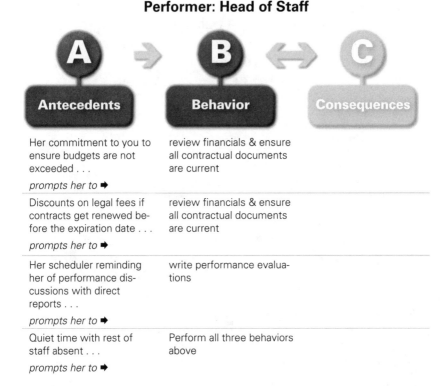

Antecedents	Behavior	Consequences
Her commitment to you to ensure budgets are not exceeded . . . *prompts her to* ➡	review financials & ensure all contractual documents are current	
Discounts on legal fees if contracts get renewed before the expiration date . . . *prompts her to* ➡	review financials & ensure all contractual documents are current	
Her scheduler reminding her of performance discussions with direct reports . . . *prompts her to* ➡	write performance evaluations	
Quiet time with rest of staff absent . . . *prompts her to* ➡	Perform all three behaviors above	

Those **Antecedents** prompt her behavior, but what *keeps it going* are the **Consequences:**

- Each time she completes a budget review, she knows she is ensuring that the company's expenses are on track. This to her is **Encouraging** so she continues to complete the budget reviews (her behavior increases).

- She has often helped people improve performance and further their careers by giving them feedback. They value this greatly, and she values helping them. She looks forward to meeting and hearing how things are going from their perspective. This to her is **Encouraging**—so she continues writing performance reviews (her behavior increases).

- Every time she reviews the dateline on legal contracts, her pleasure grows, because she is increasing the likelihood of finding contracts that are not yet past their expiration date. To her, this is **Encouraging**–so she keeps reviewing contracts (her behavior increases). Here is an ABC analysis showing these consequences and the result:

Performer: Head of Staff

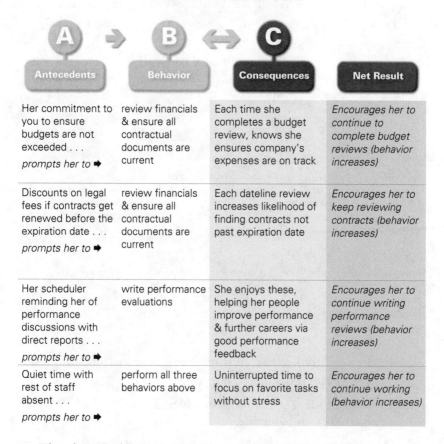

Antecedents	Behavior	Consequences	Net Result
Her commitment to you to ensure budgets are not exceeded . . . *prompts her to* ➡	review financials & ensure all contractual documents are current	Each time she completes a budget review, knows she ensures company's expenses are on track	*Encourages her to continue to complete budget reviews (behavior increases)*
Discounts on legal fees if contracts get renewed before the expiration date . . . *prompts her to* ➡	review financials & ensure all contractual documents are current	Each dateline review increases likelihood of finding contracts not past expiration date	*Encourages her to keep reviewing contracts (behavior increases)*
Her scheduler reminding her of performance discussions with direct reports . . . *prompts her to* ➡	write performance evaluations	She enjoys these, helping her people improve performance & further careers via good performance feedback	*Encourages her to continue writing performance reviews (behavior increases)*
Quiet time with rest of staff absent . . . *prompts her to* ➡	perform all three behaviors above	Uninterrupted time to focus on favorite tasks without stress	*Encourages her to continue working (behavior increases)*

The lesson here is simple: *encouraging (positive) consequences increase behavior!*

Decreasing Behavior. What would happen if she went to review budgets, but no current financial data was on file? She might search her e-mail and review the financial program, but to her this would be **Discouraging**—so she would soon quit out of frustration (and start calling the CFO or controller!). Her behavior of reviewing financial reports would decrease—and stop altogether, temporarily.

What would happen if HR delayed all performance reviews for three months? This to her would be **Discouraging**—so her behavior of writing reviews would likely decrease (at least temporarily!). Here is an ABC analysis showing these consequences and the result:

Performer: Head of Staff

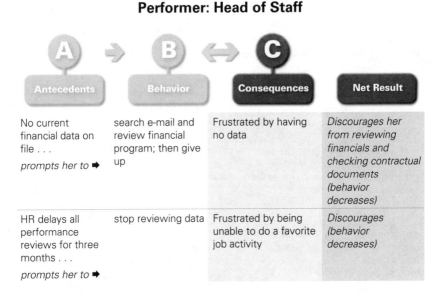

Antecedents	Behavior	Consequences	Net Result
No current financial data on file . . . *prompts her to* ➡	search e-mail and review financial program; then give up	Frustrated by having no data	*Discourages her from reviewing financials and checking contractual documents (behavior decreases)*
HR delays all performance reviews for three months . . . *prompts her to* ➡	stop reviewing data	Frustrated by being unable to do a favorite job activity	*Discourages (behavior decreases)*

Research on goal-setting and feedback demonstrates the relative power of antecedents and consequences:

- An **Antecedent** alone will produce a small, often temporary change in behavior.
- A **Consequence** alone will produce modest, lasting changes in behavior.
- But **Antecedents** backed up by **Consequences** that are immediate will produce the greatest changes in behavior (either increase or decrease).

Our experience in applying Behavioral Science in corporate settings corroborates these findings over and over again.

Consequences Rule: 4x Greater Impact on Behavior Than Antecedents

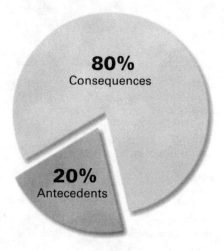

Ironically, leaders spend significantly more of their time and resources in the wrong place—on antecedents! They deliver vision statements, restructure staff and work processes, and provide training—all of which are important antecedents to prompt the right behavior. But they leave the critical **consequences** of behaviors unattended!

To me, it's like watching a gambler put 80% of his cash on a good-looking horse that can't run very well! This may make for an enjoyable day at the races, but it's not a good way to make money.

Below are two ABC analysis tables that illustrate the relative power of antecedents and consequences. The first table shows consequences that *discourage* behavior.

Consequences That DISCOURAGE Behavior

A → Antecedents	B ↔ Behavior	C Consequences	Net Result
Manager asks for input . . . *which prompts* ➡	employee to share idea—but Manager takes a call while employee is talking	So, employee feels ignored and stops sharing idea.	*Discourages performer from sharing ideas*
Customer smells fresh baked goods in bakery . . . *which prompts* ➡	customer to ask employee to warm a muffin—but employee rolls eyes, says others are waiting	So, unhappy customer leaves.	*Discourages customer from buying*
Employee is trained to smile and greet customer . . . *which prompts* ➡	employee smiles, says to customer, "How are you?"— but impatient customer says, "Why do you care?"	So, employee's feelings are hurt.	*Discourages employee from smiling and greeting customers*
Employee is trained to suggest using *company* credit card . . . *which prompts* ➡	employee to suggest using *company* card when she sees customer using different card—but customer scowls, "Don't push stuff at me!"	So, employee's feelings are hurt.	*Discourages employee from suggesting company card*
Sales reps told to jointly call on customers . . . *which prompts* ➡	Rep A (has serviced account for 3 years) to invite Rep B on joint call—but customer buys 80% from Rep B and 20% from A	So, Rep A's commission is reduced by 80%.	*Discourages Rep A from working with another rep again*

On the other hand, **Consequences** can *encourage* desired behaviors. This chart shows consequences that *encourage* behavior.

Consequences That ENCOURAGE Behavior

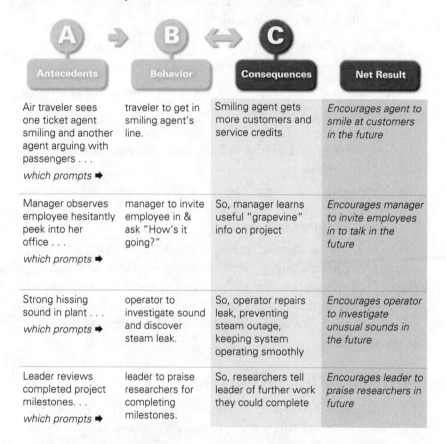

Antecedents	Behavior	Consequences	Net Result
Air traveler sees one ticket agent smiling and another agent arguing with passengers . . . *which prompts* ➡	traveler to get in smiling agent's line.	Smiling agent gets more customers and service credits	*Encourages agent to smile at customers in the future*
Manager observes employee hesitantly peek into her office . . . *which prompts* ➡	manager to invite employee in & ask "How's it going?"	So, manager learns useful "grapevine" info on project	*Encourages manager to invite employees in to talk in the future*
Strong hissing sound in plant . . . *which prompts* ➡	operator to investigate sound and discover steam leak.	So, operator repairs leak, preventing steam outage, keeping system operating smoothly	*Encourages operator to investigate unusual sounds in the future*
Leader reviews completed project milestones. . . *which prompts* ➡	leader to praise researchers for completing milestones.	So, researchers tell leader of further work they could complete	*Encourages leader to praise researchers in future*

Clearly, a good leader can make a big difference by *managing consequences* for employees—particularly when the naturally occurring consequences are undesirable, and thus require action.

THE BEST LEADERS ARE GOOD MANAGERS OF CONSEQUENCES

The effect of every consequence is either encouraging or discouraging. So the balance of encouragers to discouragers will tell you whether a behavior is likely to recur:

- More **Encouragers** mean more likely recurrence.
- More **Discouragers** mean less likely recurrence.

And there are additional variables that amplify or diminish the impact of a consequence:

- Consequences that happen right away, are important to the person, and are likely, will have maximum impact on future behavior.
- Conversely—consequences that are delayed, matter little to the performer, and are unlikely, will have much less effect on future behavior.

So, note to leaders: Creating a want-to environment that engages employees and promotes greater discretionary performance is one where the performer experiences encouraging consequences that are immediate, important to them, and occur reliably, over and over. *To be a leader is to be a good manager of consequences.*

CONSEQUENCE ANALYSIS

To understand how a consequence affects behavior, extend the ABC analysis by adding a more detailed Consequence Analysis:

Consequence Analysis . . .

. . . analyzes the Effect of consequences upon the performer, to understand which consequences are most likely to Encourage or Discourage recurrence of behavior.

E-TIP Analysis™ Reveals Impact of Each Consequence

Because consequences are all about **Effect,** you can determine if behavior is more or less likely to happen again by examining the Encouragers and Discouragers that follow it. All consequences are not, however, created equal. Our company teaches the E-TIP Analysis™ to clients as a way to know which Encouragers or Discouragers are going to have the most effect. The E-TIP Analysis asks about **Timing, Importance,** and **Probability.**

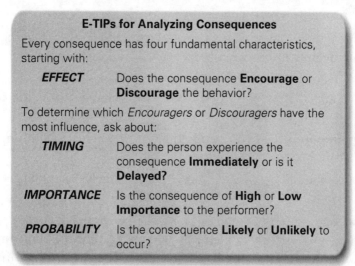

E-TIPs for Analyzing Consequences

Every consequence has four fundamental characteristics, starting with:

EFFECT	Does the consequence **Encourage** or **Discourage** the behavior?

To determine which *Encouragers* or *Discouragers* have the most influence, ask about:

TIMING	Does the person experience the consequence **Immediately** or is it **Delayed?**
IMPORTANCE	Is the consequence of **High** or **Low** Importance to the performer?
PROBABILITY	Is the consequence **Likely** or **Unlikely** to occur?

Here's how to use the **E-TIP Analysis** to understand consequences in depth. To the standard ABC analysis (Antecedent–Behavior–Consequence), just add columns to the right to indicate Effect, Timing, Importance, Probability:

A → B ↔ C	Consequence Analysis (E-TIP)			
Antecedents / Behavior / Consequences	**EFFECT** on behavior (Encourage, Discourage)	**TIMING** (Immediate, Delayed	**IMPOR-TANCE** to performer (High, Low)	**PROBA-BILITY** (Likely, Unlikely)

In doing this analysis, *step into the performer's shoes.* It's not how you see the consequences—*it's how the performer experiences them.*

First, for each consequence, observe or ask the performer:

- **Effect**—Does the performer experience this consequence as **Encouraging** or **Discouraging?**

The impact of consequences on behavior is very predictable. If there are more Encouragers than Discouragers, the person is probably going to do the same behavior again. On the other hand, more Discouragers than Encouragers means the person will probably stop doing the behavior.

To figure out which of several consequences are going to have the most influence, observe or ask the performer:

- **Timing**—Does the performer experience the consequence **Immediately** upon performing the behavior, or is the consequence **Delayed?**

- **Importance**—Is the consequence of **High** or **Low** importance to the performer?

- **Probability**—Is the Consequence **Likely** or **Unlikely** to occur?

Be very open in examining how the performer would experience a consequence. Sometimes, what is best for the company is not best for the individual . . . and vice versa. To help performers change their behaviors, introduce consequences that happen right away, are important to the performer, and are consistently applied.

Applying E-TIP Analysis to Our SellMation Example

Returning to the frustrated salespeople who had to stop calling CSRs and log in for order entry and pricing . . . let's analyze the consequences in their situation.

Consequence Analysis: Sales Reps Log Onto Network

A → B ↔ C Antecedents / Behavior / Consequences			Consequence Analysis (E-TIP)			
Antecedents	Behavior	Consequences	EFFECT on behavior (Encourage, Discourage)	TIMING (Immediate, Delayed	IMPOR-TANCE to performer (High, Low)	PROBA-BILITY (Likely, Unlikely)
CSRs no longer enter orders, provide pricing, support sales reps, *which prompts* ➡	Sales reps to log onto network to place orders and get pricing	More time, hassle	DIScourage	Immediate	High	Likely
Sales reps trained to log onto system, *which prompts* ➡		Fewer sales calls in a day	DIScourage	Delayed	High	Likely
		Uncomfortable using computer; get lost in program	DIScourage	Immediate	High	Likely
Supervisor memo reminds reps to use accurate pricing, *which prompts* ➡		Hard to access Internet	DIScourage	Immediate	High	Likely
		Get pricing 24/7	ENcourage	Immediate	High	Likely

The situation seems grim: mostly discouraging consequences, most of which are immediate, important, and tend to happen consistently, with decrease in the desired behavior. One way to help is to create encouraging consequences for the salespeople, to encourage the new behavior of logging in.

In fact, a proactive leader who knew Behavioral Science would anticipate the discouraging consequences for salespeople, and plan encouraging consequences *before* implementing the new system.

So, let's try it. Add a new antecedent—and most important, powerful new consequences—that will encourage the new behaviors:

NEW Consequence Analysis:
Sales Reps Log Onto Network

Antecedents	Behavior	Consequences	Consequence Analysis (E-TIP)			
			EFFECT on behavior (Encourage, Discourage)	TIMING (Immediate, Delayed	IMPOR-TANCE to performer (High, Low)	PROBA-BILITY (Likely, Unlikely)
Communi-cation to salespeople detailing program's expected cost savings & how they will be applied . . . which prompts ➡	Reps to log onto network to place orders, get pricing	New commission structure allows fewer sales calls	ENcourage	Delayed	High	Likely
		Better product info to customers	ENcourage	Immediate	High	Likely
		Competitors can't give customers info this fast	ENcourage	Immediate	High	Likely
		Less paperwork allows add'l day for calls every 2 weeks	ENcourage	Delayed	High	Likely
		Customers praise better service	ENcourage	Delayed	High	Likely
		Salespeople see updates while logged on	ENcourage	Immediate	High	Likely

This case demonstrates how behavioral changes that are driven by technology and process can have negative consequences for users. But if you understand the consequences that drive old behaviors, and the consequences needed to shape new behaviors, you can smooth the transition and achieve better performance.

It comes down to consequences, especially those that are **Encouraging, Immediate, Highly Important** to the performer, and **Likely** to occur (E-TIP).

Sometimes negative consequences are unavoidable—like cleaning up at the end of the shift. This is yet another reason why, if the behaviors are important to the organization, it is worth your time to arrange positive consequences to mitigate the impact of negative ones.

Delivering consequences that align with desired outcomes makes all the difference.

Now you can better appreciate . . .

- Why salespeople skip out early on Friday for golf (**Encourager–Immediate–Important–Likely**), even if it means jeopardizing a sales award for the quarter (**Encourager–Delayed–Important–Likelihood unknown**)?

- Why we eat delicious chocolate brownies (**Encourager–Immediate–Important–Likely**) even though we are trying to lose weight (**Encourager–Delayed–Important–Likelihood unknown**)?

- Why kids continue to act out to get their way (**Encourager–Immediate–Important–Likely**) even as we threaten that Santa won't come if they continue to misbehave (**Discourager–Delayed–Important–Likelihood unknown**)?

We must be honest with ourselves and each other in analyzing consequences. It is not through our eyes, but through the eyes of those who experience the effects.

Immediate Encouragers are Key for Children

As parents we ask children to do many things: "Clear the table . . . pick up your room . . . study for your test . . . put away your stuff." And it easily becomes nagging. For children, the consequences are **Discouraging, Immediate,** of **Low Importance,** and **Unlikely.** No wonder they opt out.

What we have learned (through much trial and error!) is that adding **Encouraging, Immediate, Important, Likely** consequences for those same behaviors makes a difference—and the absence of them, when a child experiences **Discouraging, Immediate** consequences, is a problem!

My children prefer company when doing their chores, so I offer to help—in the early stages (**Encouraging, Immediate, Important, Likely**)—to get the behaviors going. Other times, I suggest getting a chore done so we can throw a football or kick a soccer ball around (activities they find positive). (When I say these things, I must follow through on my word, or my words will lose all credibility in the future.)

Still other times, I explain that, to have a friend over, they first must clean their room, finish their homework, whatever. I enthusiastically praise them for their efforts ("Hey—that room is looking AWESOME!")—and then deliver on my own commitment about having a friend over.

TAKEAWAYS ON THE ABC'S

At this milestone, you've learned key foundation pieces. Here are takeaways from this chapter:

1. To proactively manage behavior and create business results, understand the influences on behavior. The ABC analysis is your tool for understanding behavior (ABCs = Antecedents ➤ Behavior ⬅➤ Consequences) and is at the center of **Activate & Consequate.**

2. Once you have pinpointed the Behavior, there are three remaining steps in an ABC analysis:

- Identify **Antecedents**—events that come before behavior and prompt it to occur.

- Identify **Consequences**—events that follow behavior and influence whether it will recur.

- Conduct a **consequence analysis** (E-TIP):

  • **Effect:** Encouraging or Discouraging

  • **Timing:** Immediate or Delayed

  • **Importance:** High or Low

  • **Probability:** Likely or Unlikely

3. Consequences are far more powerful than Antecedents when it comes to long-term effects on Behavior. If you are going to invest in Behavior, invest heavily in encouraging Consequences. And make sure your Consequences support your Antecedents and do not conflict.

4. Consequences that are Encouraging, Immediate, Highly Important, and Likely—from the performer's viewpoint—are the most powerful. Find all the Encouragers you can for a behavior, because they lead to far greater discretionary performance.

Because consequences are such an important part of the whole equation, we will explore them further in the next chapter.

Highlighting Excellence . . .

ABCs at Canadian National Railway Score Major Savings

In a few short years, Canadian National Railway has gone from a traditional railroad with classic issues to the highest-performing major freight rail service in North America. Underlying this dramatic culture change is the "ABCs," their name for applied Behavioral Science. Les Dakens, SVP of People, explains: "Company-wide, all CN leaders and managers have learned to apply the ABCs to better-manage the daily reality of moving millions of tons of commodities."

This story is about risk management: about reducing the cost of damage to the thousands of intermodal containers ("containerized shipping") that we see in shipyards, on tractor-trailers, and on hundreds of CN's trains. Gordon Trafton, SVP of CN's Southern Region, notes: "Cost control is one of CN's five guiding principles—any time we can reduce unnecessary costs safely, that savings drops straight to the bottom line."

"Intermodal containers lead a rough life," says George Greanias, CLG's Project Manager. "As in any shipping, when a container is damaged, the responsible party pays the bill. This is a high cost, a risk that every rail carrier works to minimize by spotting damage to units as they come in the gate on trucks. *Through applying the ABCs, CN is winning this battle to the tune of an astonishing quarter-million dollars a month—and that is in just one of their locations."*

CN's Bruce Bierman, General Manager at the intermodal yard in Chicago, reports: "At this yard, CN inspectors report damage to containers and trailers after they arrive by truck to CN's terminal. If we don't capture this damage on arrival—if we accept the equipment as 'good'—it makes us liable for any repair costs.

"We examine incoming containers with video cameras. Inspectors watch the monitors and complete damage reports. Despite this, in the first half of 2004, CN had the highest liability exposure of any rail line in Chicago: we were identifying very little damage, saving only $4,000–5,000 a month."

"Then, in June 2004, a small CN team used the ABC tools to explore the issue. They guided inspectors to better observe, identify, and record damage, and provided training to improve their camera observations. We also implemented a process change to allow inspectors to better capture the information without unnecessary delay to arriving trucks."

CLG consultant Jack Hinzman says, "The supervisors identified gaps and coached employees on which areas needed improvement. They discussed the results with each inspector to ensure they realized the value of their efforts."

As Bruce Bierman proudly notes, *"The result was that inspectors began capturing, on average, six times more damage. CN quickly went from worst to best in Chicago. And we recognized the inspectors for their efforts.*

"We continued these great results for 12 months. But in May 2005, results began to slide. So we revisited processes and behaviors to determine why.

"Our team then implemented a behavior change: in addition to the camera observations, inspectors also walked around arriving trucks to make a physical inspection. This helped them identify more damage that was not always visible with the cameras.

"This change generated significant bottom-line results: we went from the original six-fold improvement to a fifty-fold improvement, exceeding $250,000 in savings monthly."

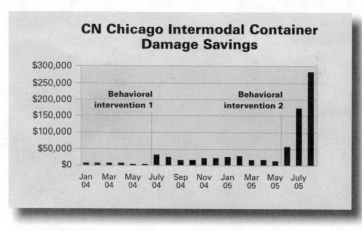

"Knowing that a physical inspection may uncover damage that is not readily evident from cameras, employees now make the call on whether to perform a physical inspection in addition to using cameras. Supervisors give inspectors encouraging feedback and celebrate their success. And employees have taken a lead in maintaining this important savings trend. The ABC approach has played a critical role in making the Chicago team into more effective performers and leaders."

Chicago Terminal Manager Steve Serio notes, "When the Intermodal team learned about the ABCs, we saw right away that we could take some of our stagnant processes and make them work better by changing our key behaviors. The proof is in the results."

CHAPTER

4

It's a Matter of Consequences

"I have three children. My wife was pregnant with our fourth. I had received two promotions in three years and was now the Head of Strategy, reporting to the Chairman/CEO. He called me into his office and said they needed me to move to Brussels to lead our European division. It meant a promotion to SVP, more pay and stock options, etc.

"But it also meant relocation, more travel, my children changing schools, and my wife losing her support system. So I declined the offer—even knowing that in our company's culture it might mean that I'd be passed over for future promotions. But I was OK with that."

—*SVP of Strategy & Growth,*
Fortune 100 Company

UNDERSTANDING how consequences influence behavior is critical to understanding why we do what we do—and how to change our own behavior. To review quickly, *consequences* are events or conditions that follow a behavior. They either encourage or discourage the behavior from occurring again.

As the story above points out, consequences are powerful. The SVP was faced with consequences that drove his behavior. The **Encouraging** consequences to him were promotion, more pay, etc. But the **Discouraging** consequences were relocation, more travel, and impacts upon his family. So his behavior was to decline the opportunity.

Understanding how consequences influence behavior is critical to understanding why you and I do what we do—and therefore is the key to changing behavior.

INCREASING BEHAVIOR OR DECREASING BEHAVIOR?

Behavioral analysis involves breaking behavior and its surrounding environment into components. In particular, we use the ABC analysis to understand behavior in terms of its antecedents and consequences. The result is a different view of the world—one that provides objective clues to why we behave as we do.

The following examples show chains of typical everyday behavior broken down into individual *behaviors* (**B**) and *consequences* (**C**). These examples demonstrate why specific behaviors increase or decrease . . .

- You use a new web search engine (**B**) and find information faster than with the engine you were using (**C**). *(This positive consequence encourages your behavior of using that new search engine again.)*
- A child touches a hot stove (**B**) and gets burned (**C**). *(This negative consequence discourages the behavior of touching hot stoves!)*

- You drive 60 mph in a 30-mph zone **(B)** and get a ticket, complete with points and fees **(C)**. *(Getting a ticket, paying the fine, and getting points on your license are all negative consequences that will discourage your behavior of speeding, particularly when a police officer is present (A).)*

- You go into the office early **(B)** because you want to avoid being unprepared for a meeting with your boss **(C)**. *(You will likely do that again in the future, if the preparation time helps make the meeting more successful.)*

- You connect to Amazon.com **(B)**, quickly find the book you are looking for **(C)**, and order it easily **(B)** without having to leave your home **(C)**. *(You will likely use amazon.com again in the future. There is a business lesson here.)*

- You work extra time on a special report for your team **(B)**, get it to them on time **(B)**, but hear no feedback at all **(C)**. *(Your behavior of working "extra time" probably will not occur the next time they ask.)*

Once a behavior starts, its consequences determine whether or not it will continue.

Usually, knowing that a consequence is encouraging or discouraging is sufficient for an ABC analysis. But to plan the most effective consequences, you need to know some subtler aspects of Encouragers and Discouragers.

LEADERS ARE DEFINED BY THE CONSEQUENCES THEY CHOOSE

Your consequence "style" defines your leadership.

If you manage primarily through discouraging consequences or coercion, employees learn quickly to do only what they have to—comply just enough to avoid negative consequences.

The flogging will continue until morale improves

Contrast this with a leader who provides encouraging consequences for desired behavior. Employees fortunate enough to work for this type of leader will perform above and beyond the base level of expectation, because they want to. *This is the simple secret to engaging employees and unleashing discretionary performance in your organization! Focus on catching people doing things right—and let them know their efforts are appreciated.*

Employees seek opportunities to work with leaders who are positive and encouraging. This creates a cumulative effect for both types of leaders: positive leaders become more effective because they get more support, and negative leaders grow less effective because their people are less productive and do not give discretionary effort.

In reality, leaders mix consequences. The real issue is how they *balance* them. Many leaders think they are positive managers, but actually use threats or fear as their primary leadership style. Here are "leading indicators" that a leader may be operating in a more fear-based way:

- Inability to retain strong talent
- Premature leveling-off (not being promoted)
- Employees transferring internally from leader's department to others, with few-to-none choosing to transfer in.

Avoid "Great, But" Leadership

People listen carefully to leaders, and one thing they listen for is *"great, but"* statements. The "great" is encouraging and positive . . . however, if followed by "but," people know that a negative is coming. This is a classic mistake made by leaders who don't understand behavior.

It's like a good news/bad news joke: "The good news is that production doubled last month—but the bad news is you were on vacation." The bad news sharply undercuts the good news.

Here's a real example of a CFO who hurt his leadership with "great, but" statements, as told by one of my colleagues:

I was hired to coach Carlos, who had a great record as CFO. Everyone said, "You won't have to coach him—he has it all down." So I hoped for the best, and scheduled coaching sessions and chances to observe Carlos in team meetings.

At first, Carlos did seem to have it all down. His meetings were well-organized, and he often commented on the good things he heard or saw as his team reported progress.

Then I began to notice a subtle behavior pattern. Several times during the meeting, Carlos would stop, summarize the successes, and congratulate the team. Then he would say something like this:

"We had a great month, and I am looking forward to another one. All of you have done a wonderful job, and I congratulate you. This is *great, but* we are not across the finish line. We have to do what we did this month and more to make our quarterly numbers, and the next quarter is even more challenging. Celebrate, your work is *great, but* we have a lot to do."

I quickly looked around the room and observed the faces. Like many of us during a long week, they showed the signs of stress. But something else was there. Despite success, the team seemed down. I stayed after the meeting to ask a couple of team members for their reactions.

They both said, "Carlos is never satisfied. His stretch goals grow higher and higher. The pressure is subtle, but always there. The only relief was when quarterly results went 20% above goal."

So I saw Carlos for our regular coaching session. I described what I had observed in the meeting, and the impact of his behavior on the team. He looked shocked and told me his version.

"I want to be positive. I tell them how much I appreciate what they do. I really *do* appreciate it, you know. *But* I just can't seem to trust that they won't let down their guard. I guess I'm afraid that they will take my positive feedback to mean they can relax. *But* I can never relax—*they* can never relax—*we* can

never relax. It is a competitive world. I have to live with it, and so do they!*"*

Carlos' *"great, but"* behavior in verbal communication is one of the most frequent missteps leaders exhibit. In an effort to avoid misrepresenting a situation, and not to leave people feeling that they can become complacent, leaders (and parents!) have a tendency to say things like . . .

- "Great job organizing the celebration with our key customers, *but* I expected more of them to show up."
- "Our first quarter was on target and on budget, *but* I'm not sure we'll be able to pull it off two quarters in a row."
- "I'm pleased with your performance overall, *but* it's not quite where you need it to be if we're going to promote you. Keep up the great work—*but* you need to try harder."
- "I'm really proud of you, sweetheart. A 96% on your geometry test is a super grade. *But* what happened to the other four points?"

A way around the *"great, but"* is to separate your feedback with some time, if possible. At the very least, you need to separate your statements. Here are a couple of the examples from above, reworked:

"Great, but" version: "Great job organizing the celebration with our key customers, *but* I expected more of them to show up."

Preferred: "Great job organizing the celebration with our key customers! I was very pleased with how it turned out. Did you expect that number of attendees? I thought the theme was just excellent and the booths were very effective for showcasing our new products . . ."

"Great, but" version: "Our first quarter was on target and on budget, *but* I'm not sure we'll be able to pull it off two quarters in a row."

Preferred: "We did a wonderful job during the first quarter. Our performance was on target and on budget, which pleased me greatly. This quarter is going to be a tough one, though. I know it will take everyone's maximum efforts to hit our numbers. How are you all feeling about it?"

A Lesson to Remember

The story and examples above have a hidden lesson. People who provide *consequences* for behavior—are also *impacted* themselves! Carlos the CFO very much wanted to reinforce his team's efforts that led to great results, although he needed to challenge them to work even harder. As a result of his "great, but" statements, the team actually felt their behavior was being punished.

No matter how hard they worked, they felt they couldn't please Carlos and couldn't receive positive consequences for their efforts. And what Carlos did not realize was that his pattern of providing "great, but" consequences was damaging his team's morale and perception of him. And that, in turn, was a strong discouraging consequence for Carlos!

It's a Matter of When, Not If

As a leader, are there times when you should use harsher consequences/discouragement? Absolutely—especially if you need to influence a behavior very quickly. Negative consequences are appropriate when you see someone engaging in dangerous or illegal behavior, or when there is something truly bad happening that must be immediately stopped. It also might be appropriate if an employee is systematically undermining an important initiative or work process.

FOUR WAYS TO DELIVER CONSEQUENCES

How consequences are delivered may surprise you. There are obvious ways, like praise, hockey tickets, or a reprimand. But behavioral scientists cluster consequences into four categories, based on how they are delivered:

1. *Feedback Consequences*—words of praise, applause, frowns, smiles, measurement data that allow performance evaluation, etc.

2. *Tangible Consequences*—desirable physical items like money, plaques, letters of commendation, tickets, etc.

3. *Activity Consequences*—the opportunity to participate in an activity that is rewarding to the performer, like preferred work activities, company-sponsored softball, conference attendance, training, etc.

4. *Work Process Consequences*—the steps in a work process actually encourage or discourage behavior that must occur to complete the process. If the steps make it easier or more fun to complete the process, they are encouragers. If the steps make it harder to complete the process, they are discouragers.

Let us look at how each of the four types is delivered.

1. Feedback Consequences

Feedback is information given to the performer about a behavior or the behavior's result. In the context of ABC analysis, giving feedback means providing information to a person that enables him/her to adjust their behavior. Such feedback can be positive or constructive:

- *Positive feedback* gives people words of praise and commendation that encourage their repeating the desired behaviors in the future.

- *Constructive feedback* has two parts: information to discourage an undesirable behavior, and information to encourage a different, more preferred behavior.

Positive feedback is generally easy for most of us to deliver— "You did a great job getting that report out on time!" However, it is tough for some. We have worked with leaders who believe that positive feedback misleads people into thinking they've done enough and need not do more. Others believe that people who need positive feedback are weak. Still others believe that people know what they need to do and don't need feedback about their performance. Whatever their reasoning, these managers are not comfortable delivering positive feedback, so they rarely provide it.

For most of us, delivering *constructive feedback* is more challenging because we fear that the receiver "might not take it well," leading to an uncomfortable confrontation. But proper constructive feedback involves pinpointing the behaviors we wish to discourage, while also pinpointing more preferred behaviors.

Constructive feedback *can* be done well, with grace and style. It can leave the receiver quite confident and able to change his or her behavior. And it can leave the giver feeling good about it too.

We have found that the most effective feedback, whether positive or constructive, is NORMS-based. Remember that NORMS helps you state your observations about behavior objectively, as shown here:

NORMS of Objectivity™

Not an Interpretation

Observable

Reliable

Measurable

Specific

We saw a wonderful example of constructive feedback when a manager spoke to a direct report following a meeting on discretionary bonuses . . .

George, I wanted to share some feedback on the meeting. Having participated in these sessions for three years, I can say it was our best yet! We had everyone there, which required good scheduling on your end. Plus, the questions sent in advance allowed everyone to be a meaningful contributor. I think that went a long way.

> One thing I would do differently next time is to ask people to put in writing who they felt should receive bonuses and why. When we went around the table, some people went on and on, while others had no data to back up their recommendations. It struck me that we never specified what we wanted them to tell us about their nominees.
>
> To ensure it doesn't degrade into a popularity contest, maybe we could add a template to our pre-work that would clearly specify what data we were seeking—and would serve as a prompt for folks to submit the data in advance. What do you think?

This manager did an effective job pinpointing what went well, what didn't go so well, and what she would prefer to see done in the future. The feedback was objective and NORMS-based, not personal. The manager used "we" to share ownership of the situation, rather than blaming George for any problems. Finally, she asked questions, rather than acting like "the expert." As a result, George felt good about the session and knew precisely what to do next year.

This recalls another story from my colleague Denny Sullivan. He was coaching a young, high-potential leader, Johnny, who had incredible skill at giving constructive feedback. Johnny's direct reports bragged about him, saying he made clear what they were doing incorrectly, and was always clear and specific on what he wanted them to do differently in the future. Further, he did this in a non-emotional, yet caring way.

Denny was struck by the respect these older direct reports had for their young new boss. The direct reports confided in Denny that for over twenty years, they hadn't known what they were doing wrong—just that they always got average performance reviews from their (former) bosses. But since Johnny became their supervisor, that all changed—mostly because he was so skilled at coaching them on improvement areas and then being sure to praise them when they did things correctly.

We'll talk a lot more about feedback, both positive and constructive, in Chapter 5.

2. Tangible Consequences

Tangible consequences can be physically touched and held. They include trophies, pictures, mugs, commendation letters, money, movie tickets, nicer offices, lunch, etc. Tangible items are ubiquitous in corporate settings, especially if they carry the company logo.

Tangible consequences can be very effective—*if they are seen as positive by the receivers*. One needs to be careful here. For example, we saw one meeting where, to recognize record quarterly sales, the top 200 sellers received tickets to a hot Broadway show.

A few really liked this gift, but most did not. Instead of positively receiving the tickets, they grumbled, "I'd rather have the $250" or "Who came up with this harebrained reward?" Thus a tangible consequence meant to recognize top performers backfired, having a negative effect on many in the group.

So, tangible encouragers are tricky. The key thing to remember is that "beauty is in the eye of the beholder," or in behavioral terms, "an encourager depends on what the receiver values."

And a tangible item acts as an encourager only if the encouraged behavior continues. One size does *not* fit all, and tangible consequences for one group could be judged as junk by others. An easy solution here is to just ask employees what tangible items they would enjoy.

3. Activity Consequences

The power of *activity consequences* has long been known by parents and grandparents the world over. "Would you like dessert? You have to eat your peas." "Want to go outside to play? Finish your homework." "You'd like to invite your friends for a sleepover tomorrow night? Please clean your room first."

In business, activity consequences can work the same way. Some people enjoy brainstorming; others hate it. Some enjoy working out project details; others prefer to focus on the big issues. So, an employee's favorite activity—such as being part of a planning team—will encourage a less-preferred one, like preparing audit materials. Long ago, behavioral scientists discovered that an easy, preferred task will encourage the completion of a harder, less-preferred task.

One supervisor we know had a telemarketing team of a dozen. They cold-called all day—discouraging work, as few contacts resulted in a sale. Then the supervisor discovered that the telemarketers preferred working on special teams more than their daily work. In fact, so many in her group signed up for special teams that properly staffing her shifts became difficult.

She could have decided to participate on the special teams herself, which would have forced the telemarketers to stay at their desks. But this wise supervisor went for a win-win. She made participating on special teams contingent upon telemarketing activities. In other words, telemarketers had access to a preferred task (participating on special teams) based on their performance on a less-preferred task (making cold calls). She saw gains in productivity, and employees were happy because they continued to participate on special teams.

4. Consequences Provided Through Work Processes

Much of the work that occurs in organizations follows a process—a series of steps that, when complete, produces an outcome. Sometimes processes are easy to follow and make people's lives easier. Sometimes they make people's lives miserable. In each case, consequences are clearly at work.

Consequences are embedded in every step of work processes. If performers experience encouragement by completing a process step, they will find the work process more rewarding. If they experience discouragement, they will find it difficult to complete the work process. Many things in your daily life reflect this basic truth.

Remember our salespeople from SellMation? The new work process made it harder for them to enter orders—thus discouraging their behavior of "following the process." When people experience discouragers like this, they often create workarounds—in the SellMation case, they called the CSR anyway.

Our local photo processing center provides a wonderful example of a work process that makes it easier to complete a task: printing digital photos. All you do is upload your photos to the center's website (where it recognizes your email address, name, billing structure, and development preferences.) Three mouse clicks and one hour later, your printed photos are ready for pick-up.

This occurs through a thoughtfully structured work process. Your behavior of uploading your digital photos to their website is encouraged through work process consequences they have structured: **Encouraging, Immediate, Important, Likely.** (This is a good lesson for businesses to heed: fill work processes with encouragers to get the processes used.)

ALIGNING CONSEQUENCES

A common issue we see in companies is consequence systems that are misaligned, or not aligned at all. An example is re-designing work processes to promote teamwork, but keeping tangible rewards individualized.

Another example: equipment failure potentially costs a company millions, so a supervisor encourages preventive maintenance and proactive intervention to prevent failure—but receives negative consequences at bonus time, because his quarterly expenses exceed the allotted maintenance budget.

For your company to succeed, align the consequences for behaviors you need. Otherwise, you will be led into antecedent-based fixes to correct a problem that ultimately lies in the consequence systems.

Here's a quick test to see if your department's or company's consequence systems are aligned. Just answer *yes* or *no* to each . . .

1. My employees receive positive feedback and tangible rewards for putting in time, rather than for exhibiting desired behaviors.

2. My employees can engage in preferred activities by avoiding or handing off less-preferred activities without experiencing negative consequences.

3. I deliver tangible rewards, such as trips and tickets, for desired behaviors without consulting employees as to their preferred rewards.

4. Our "vision statement" or "values for the organization" conflicts with how employees are paid or recognized.

A "yes" to any item is a red flag that you most likely have a misalignment between the behaviors you desire and the consequences that drive behavior. This misalignment can create inconsistent behavior patterns that are hard to change unless the consequences are aligned.

WHICH CONSEQUENCES DO YOU GIVE PEOPLE?

The typical corporate leader relies on consequences such as bonuses, promotions, and reward systems to recognize desired behaviors. These consequences usually require little personal effort to deliver.

Leaders who rely on these positive consequences are underestimating the power and effect of *their words* and *their behaviors* on others. Money and promotions may be an important motivator for some behaviors, but research tells us over and over again that, while money is a necessary encourager for us to work at all, it is not sufficient to motivate us to higher levels of performance. Feedback, especially from supervisors and peers, is the way to motivate our highest levels of performance.

This is why it is so important to seize the opportunity to encourage specific behaviors that are important to you and to the success of your organization. Get out and talk with your people. *Work with them to identify the consequences that will increase the key behaviors they need to perform to attain your desired business results.*

Here is a wonderful example from Don Hamm, President and CEO of Assurant Health, that demonstrates "the power of you" . . .

> Until recently, our 3,000 nationwide employees had little sense of where the company was going, how we planned to get there, and their personal role in the process. So my team and I created a vision for the future—"Journey to Greatness"—and mapped a business strategy, including how to create the right culture.
>
> Developing the business strategy was straightforward. The harder part was the people part, and creating the right culture—something that would sustain the organization. To make that happen, we relied heavily on behavioral thinking.
>
> Two of CLG's consultants, Ned Morse and Kathy Callahan, provided executive coaching, first for me and then all SVPs, some of whom had been with the company for years.
>
> Frankly, we had to make some changes with our senior team. I couldn't have credibility if I or my own team couldn't live our core principles—intellectual honesty, personal responsibility, and excellence—and have the right behaviors.
>
> As CEO, one of my key responsibilities is to ensure that everyone in the company knows where we are going, how we're going to get there, and the impact they can have on making it happen.
>
> So I set out to do what most CEOs would find daunting or impossible: *I committed to have a conversation with every employee—all 3,000—over the course of a year. I think people really do want to connect with their leaders, and they do want to believe that what they do is important.*
>
> In all, I held more than 175 meetings with employees in groups of 10 to 20. We opened the sessions by asking them to talk about what was happening in their areas. I then talked about our company, where we were, and where we were headed. I tailored the message to their particular department.

I sought their input, particularly in identifying consequences that would help change the key behaviors required to succeed.

It wasn't just what I said at the meetings, but also that I held them at all! It sent a very powerful message—that I respect and care about them. I think people were skeptical at first, but when people saw that I am a real person, I care about the company, and I listen to what they say—it had a tremendous impact.

Behavioral Science has made a huge difference in our organization. I have seen tremendous progress and gains in our ability to get things done. I like its analytical nature. To me, it explained a lot of things I couldn't quite grasp before. I am very much a believer. I didn't know much about Behavioral Science five years ago, and today I have seen the results and think it makes a big difference.

It has helped us develop talent, particularly in our Administrative departments. If you look at the before and after, it is a startling picture, and I really attribute most of the improvement to the behavioral work, in particular the work of Ned and Kathy, who helped us put it all into practice.

We changed our performance review process not only to include results, but to improve competencies that were driven by behaviors. It sent a message to the organization that it is not just about getting results, *but how you get them.* And that it begins with the people at the top modeling the right behaviors.

We look at the stats of our turnaround—job satisfaction, cost-effectiveness—and I'm convinced it's because of a good understanding of applying Behavioral Science.

The proof is in the pudding. Our company has conducted four employee surveys, and the last two were extremely positive. I think part of it is that sense of identifying with the organization. Since Assurant, Inc. went public in 2004, our earnings have risen dramatically. Assurant Health was previously earning $40 million, and now we are at $178 million in a competitive industry.

How to Increase Your *Encouraging Consequences*

How do you increase your use of encouraging consequences and help ensure that they have the intended positive impact?

1. **Being there helps**—Encouragement works best when delivered immediately after the behavior. Being present to observe the behavior and deliver the consequences is *Encouraging-Immediate-Highly Important*.

2. **The receiver judges impact**—The receiver of consequences is the ultimate judge of whether they are positive. Ask people how they feel about the consequences you provide. Also, watch how the person reacts to discern the impact.

3. **Consistency counts**—Be sure that the same behaviors are consistently encouraged, and that the encouragement is provided over and over and over again.

4. **Variety counts**—The same positive consequences may lose their value if delivered in the same way, over and over. Develop a suite of consequences that are likely to have positive effects, and vary the ones you use. For example, you might deliver praise by e-mail, face-to-face, or through a note.

5. **Combine short-term and long-term consequences**—Immediate consequences such as praise, public recognition, and short celebrations are more effective if they are linked to long-term consequences such as performance appraisal results, merit raises, resources for individual or team projects (e.g., computers), and broad public recognition (e.g., award at a corporate quality conference).

6. **Use a 4:1 ratio**—A good rule of thumb is to deliver four times as much positive feedback as constructive feedback. Keeping track and adjusting to maintain the ratio helps to meet this goal.

7. **Ask people what they like**—Positive consequences are any that increase the strength of a behavior, but often the effect of a consequence can't be confirmed directly. Ask people what they like and what they feel is encouraging for their behavior. Most people know what they like and are willing to talk about it.

8. **Watch carefully to create a list of positive consequences**—Nothing works better for identifying positive consequences than careful observation. Any time you are around peers, team members, or supervisors, watch for foods they like, how they use their break time, reading materials they prefer, and so on. Develop a list using your observations and surprise them by picking just the right form of encouragement to celebrate success.

9. **Teach others to praise well**—Teaching team members to use positive feedback with each other is a good way to expand its use within your team. Encourage the use of positive feedback by others.

TAKEAWAYS ON CONSEQUENCES

We've covered some very important foundation pieces—especially the role of consequences in influencing behavior. Here are the top points to take from this chapter:

1. *There is a consequence for every single behavior.* Every consequence affects behavior. We don't even need to be aware of what's going on for this influence to occur.

2. *Consequences either encourage or discourage behavior.* Encouraging consequences offer many advantages, like creating a positive work environment and tapping people's discretionary effort. Discouraging consequences can have many unwanted effects, such as performers avoiding the person who delivers such consequences.

3. *Encouragers for desired behaviors are the primary tool for unlocking discretionary performance in your organization.* Encouragers promote behaviors that lead to important business results and the desired culture.

4. *Consequences are delivered in four forms:*

    - **Feedback**—a flow of information about behavior or a result, back to the performer

    - **Tangible Items**—items that can be physically touched or held

    - **Activities**—arranging activities so that having access to an easier or preferred task is contingent upon completing a difficult or less-preferred task

    - **Work processes**—the steps in a work process encourage or discourage behavior that must occur to complete the process.

Now that you are grounded in the principles of Behavioral Science—including the importance of consequences of behavior—it's time to look at how to apply the concepts you've been reading about.

So far, our journey has taken us through I-M-P-A-C of our **IMPACT MODEL**. The next chapter, on feedback and coaching, begins our journey into the *application* of behavioral science. As we develop a plan to act on what we learned in our Activate and Consequate step, we need to rely on the most powerful consequences available for influencing behavior: feedback and coaching. Let's review those important leadership skills next.

In the next chapter—feedback and coaching—you begin to *apply* Behavioral Science. The **Activate & Consequate** step of the model focuses not only consequences, but on the power of coaching and feedback in shaping new behaviors.

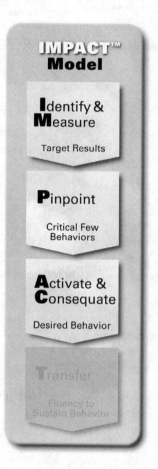

Highlighting Excellence . . .

The Personal Power of Consequences

My colleague, Dr. Karen Bush, shares a personal story that is one we all can relate to and learn from.

"**M**y doctor called after a January physical. "I have your glucose scores. Normal fasting is 70–110. Over 110, we get concerned. Yours is over 120. You are dangerously close to being Type 2 Diabetic."

I laughed. "Oh, just a fluke. Must be holiday food. There's no diabetes in my family. I'm slim and I exercise." Still, I reduced sweets in my diet. Then my doctor called after a retest three months later. "Now it's 125, and your long-term glucose is rising." Wake-up call #1.

Diabetes is a horrible disease. I can avoid it with proper diet and exercise. I educated myself about diet (using great websites, like the American Diabetes Association at http://www.diabetes.org/home.jsp), and in April began to change my diet. I cheated a bit, but there was plenty of time to bring things under control before my next blood test in August.

On Memorial Day, my plate included a hamburger, rich creamy potato salad, potato chips, baked beans full of sugary maple syrup, a slice of cake, and a slice of pie—a dreadful selection for my health. Wake-up call #2. I truly had been trying to *change my eating behavior—but my behavior hadn't changed!*

I sat in my garden room with coffee and had a little talk with myself. "This is behavior change. I am a behavioral scientist. What does my science tell me about this?" It was so simple: *it was all about consequences.* Whenever I made food choices, like the Memorial Day buffet, the powerful consequences that drove my behavior were *Encouragers–Immediate–High Importance:* that great food, plus the social interactions surrounding it.

What about my glucose? Well, yes, a bad score was a *Discourager.* But it was Delayed (several months!) and to me it was of Low Importance because I didn't fully understand the risk. Honestly, I didn't really believe diabetes would ever happen (that's called denial).

My behavioral solution was obvious: I needed *Immediate–High Importance Encouragers and Discouragers.* I needed something Immediate to tell me I was eating the right foods. Every drug store has glucose test kits that are reasonably accurate. I bought one, learned to use it, and committed to test my fasting glucose level each morning when I got up.

This gave me *feedback* on my diet for the previous day. Good food choices gave me a "normal" reading, an *Encourager* that was Immediate and became *Highly Important* to me. Poor food choices gave me a bad reading, which became a powerful *Discourager*.

Today, I am quite proud of my results. With daily feedback guiding my eating behavior, I brought my glucose levels into normal range within four weeks. And I've kept them there for over six months. It has been a fresh lesson for me in the power of consequences!"

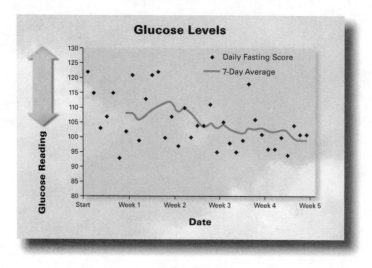

Feedback and Coaching: Putting Your "Secret Weapons" to Work!

I listened in awe as the Vice Chairman of a major oil company keynoted an international petroleum conference. He revealed the company's major strategies in intimate and remarkable detail—where they were drilling and expanding wells, seeking wealth in new areas of exploration—verging upon giving away the store, it seemed to me.

Then he revealed something even more remarkable. "What we are doing on the people side is where our real success will come from. This is how we are going to make a real difference in our performance as an organization. It is one of the most exciting things I've ever been part of.

"But you know what? I'm not going to tell you about it! The reason is because we believe it is our secret weapon."

—Leslie

THE VICE CHAIRMAN'S "secret weapon" for success was not better geology, drilling, or chemistry. He was referring to **feedback and coaching**, and he was absolutely right. They are the most underutilized levers for engaging people's hearts and minds, and tapping their discretionary performance.

Feedback is the most powerful consequence you can deliver as a leader—much more powerful than money or any other tangible—and it leads to improved, measurable results of all types.

It's a two-way street: telling someone how they did—or hearing how others view your own performance—is invaluable. It is a gift too seldom given.

> **Feedback** is information given to a person or group (e.g., team) about their behavior, and its impact.
>
> **Coaching** is working with an individual to build on the feedback to enhance performance.

Well-delivered feedback is supportive, sincere, and given with clear intent to help, not harm. The most effective leaders we know are those who give and receive feedback routinely—with great ease, frequency, and recognition of its importance and power to motivate. When done well, feedback and coaching are indeed any leader's secret weapons—shaping each individual to his/her personal best.

To encourage outstanding performance or help develop new behaviors in individuals, do three things:

- **Coach the person with objective feedback:** Use the **NORMS OF OBJECTIVITY** to describe things you have directly observed or directly heard the performer say, good or bad.

- **Coach the person by sharing the effect of their actions,** good or bad, on yourself and others in the organization. Don't leave them wondering what you think of their performance.

- Coach the person by demonstrating your desire to help and not harm.

> As a leader, you can use feedback and coaching as a powerful consequence to influence performance. Research has shown time and again that money is necessary but is not sufficient to motivate performance.
>
> Feedback, especially your feedback as a leader, is the most powerful motivator of performance

It is critical that you understand the power of your feedback. It can build people up or tear them down, in part because people listen to and analyze much of what leaders say. In this chapter, we will discuss the tools for using feedback and coaching effectively. We will review proven techniques we use with executives—the same techniques you will want to use to become a champion coach who develops people by giving feedback that matters.

PERFORMANCE APPRAISALS GIVE FEEDBACK— BUT NOT ENOUGH

In most companies, performance evaluations require leaders to spend considerable time completing forms, assigning ratings, and so on. Then they hold discussions intended to be meaningful to the performers—to help them know what they are doing well, and where they need to improve. The process consumes time, and often has mixed results. It puts enormous pressure on a single session to motivate an employee and ensure the employee knows how much the company values his/her contributions. And it's done only once a year.

If done poorly, it is easy for this session to send the wrong signals, despite the good intent. The worst-case effect is that top and valued performers simply hear "Keep it up!" or "We need more of the same." And poor performers fail to understand that others view their performance as sub-par.

As our company works within and across corporations large and small, we often hear complaints related to poorly conducted performance reviews. Here are three examples:

> **My performance review was done in an elevator! My boss said I was doing a fine job and hoped I understood that she'd let me know if there were any problems. Oh . . . and she mentioned that we both were so busy that we needn't waste time going over that ridiculous HR form. We both could better spend our time on real work.**
>
> *—EVP of Marketing, Fortune 100 company*

> **I had been in this office—the Chairman/CEO's corner office— only once before I took this position—and that was when they told me I had been selected as the next CEO! I was dumbfounded. I had received no feedback in over five years. I always thought I was doing a good job, but I sure never heard words to that effect. I was never told that my contributions were valued, or that I was even considered as a candidate for a job like this!**
>
> *—CEO, Fortune 200 company*

> **I'll never forget my first performance review! I'd been here four months. My supervisor said I was doing great and everything was fine, and I was given my six-month bonus early. I was thrilled—until the next day—when our entire department received a shutdown notice, and we were all told to apply for new positions within the company! Those who couldn't find a job within six weeks would receive a severance package with one month's pay. I make six figures! This isn't supposed to happen to a graduate engineer with over ten years of experience!**
>
> *—Engineer who leads software development for technology company with a 40 P/E ratio*

These stories demonstrate needlessly lost opportunities to encourage specific behaviors of highly valued people, and to provide caring feedback useful to key performers who are capable of even more.

Since performance evaluations affect us all in a big way, let's do an E-TIP consequence analysis:

Consequences of Performance Evaluations	EFFECT ON BEHAVIOR: Encourage/ Discourage	TIMING AFTER BEHAVIOR: Immediate/ Delayed	IMPORTANCE TO PER- FORMER: High/Low	PROBA- BILITY: Likely/ Unlikely
If performance description is vague and addresses events not under performer's control . . .	Discourage	Delayed	Low	Unlikely
If evaluations did not consider antecedents or consequences . . .	Discourage	Delayed	Low	Unlikely
If information shared is tied only loosely to everyday performance . . .	Discourage	Delayed	Low	Unlikely

That's quite an indictment! Sadly, performance evaluations have relatively little influence over the day-to-day activities of employees. They are simply too far removed from where and when things happen.

Even without this consequence analysis on the effectiveness of traditional performance appraisals, effective leaders rely on annual performance reviews very little. Instead, they invest their time purposefully by providing *frequent, pinpointed feedback and coaching* to their direct reports and to the organization at large, on behaviors that are important to the organization. They know it is the best way to leverage their role and position.

HOW FEEDBACK AND COACHING LINK TO THE IMPACT™ MODEL

As a leader, you will most often use feedback to encourage or discourage behavior—which means that feedback is a *consequence*. Therefore, we make feedback part of the **Activate & Consequate** step of the IMPACT MODEL.

Of course, two-way feedback is necessary at every step of the model. On one hand, leaders must solicit feedback: "What behaviors are we tracking?" "How are we performing in those areas?" Are you incurring any obstacles to doing _____ (important behavior)?" "How can I help?" "Are you getting the support you need from the organization to sustain the improvement?" "How can I better enable the organization to achieve our goal?"

On the other hand, leaders also must give feedback to team members and colleagues on what they see and hear, every step of the way. In fact, feedback from leaders underlies every step of our **IMPACT MODEL** and of real life. Leverage feedback, your greatest asset, to the fullest.

THREE KINDS OF FEEDBACK

There are three kinds of feedback: positive, constructive, and no feedback.

Effects of Feedback

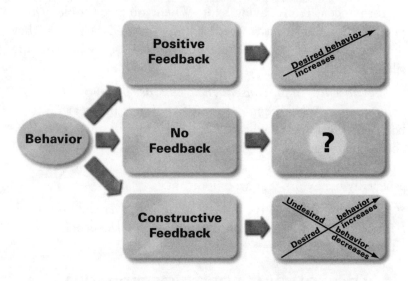

Positive feedback encourages desired behavior and makes it more likely for the behavior to happen in the future.

Constructive feedback discourages undesired behavior and encourages desired behavior (note the crossed arrows in the graphic).

When there is *no feedback,* future behavior is left up to chance. This is never good if it's a behavior that is important to your organization's success.

Often, if no positive feedback is given for effective or desired behaviors, they are likely to decrease. And if no constructive feedback is given for ineffective or inappropriate behaviors, those behaviors are likely to continue or may even increase in frequency.

*To recap: feedback is information you receive—somehow— about your behavior. Feedback is a **consequence** of your* *behavior. And feedback is most powerful when it is specific and you receive it immediately following the behavior.*

Doing Nothing . . . Is Doing Something!

In the case of feedback, not saying anything about a person's performance is really saying a lot! When you give people *neither* positive nor constructive feedback for desired behavior, they develop all sorts of (mis)interpretations about why you are silent.

The absence of a consequence can be the most powerful consequence. When people do positive things but hear no feedback or feel that what they did doesn't matter, these consequences may drive their behavior in the wrong direction! This is why you just can't leave behavior up to chance—especially behaviors that are important.

So, our number-one recommendation is to *increase your feedback, both positive and constructive.* **Don't leave behavior to chance.**

HOW DO YOU GIVE POSITIVE FEEDBACK?

It may seem obvious, but in the hustle of your hectic days, you may not think about the many ways in which you convey encouragement to others. You do it through:

- Your attention (simply spending time with someone or on a topic)
- Your words ("Excellent project summary! It is precisely what the customer asked for. Thank you!")
- Your gestures (smile, handshake, pat on the back, thumbs-up)
- Your symbols (gift, lunch, humorous award, time spent with individual, handwritten note)
- Your concern and compassion (acknowledging difficult accomplishments and challenges)
- Your actions (invitations to events, taking someone out to lunch)

All of these are ways to sincerely communicate your perception of the goodness and the contribution of behaviors you want to encourage.

We All Need Positive Feedback

So often, people assume that others do not need positive feedback. In fact, *all* of us need it. Our behavior is impacted most when we receive positive feedback promptly. The shorter the delay between behavior and feedback, the greater the impact of the feedback.

Here is a story about "Mark," a successful CEO whom I had the pleasure of coaching during his final years at the helm. At Mark's retirement dinner . . .

> One by one, direct reports and peers shared their appreciation for his leadership and entrepreneurial spirit as he led the way for corporate and industry transformation.
>
> Mark's direct reports thanked him passionately for his sensitive coaching and commitment to leadership, which he demonstrated by his relentless pursuit of continuous improvement and stretch objectives. His boss, the Board Chairman, told of the Board's faith in him and how he would be missed.
>
> After the party, I met with Mark for our final meeting pre-retirement. He shared how he was taken aback by the specific, personal, positive feedback he received at the dinner from all levels of the organization. *Then he told me that aside from what I had collected in my interviews about him at the start of our coaching relationship, he had received virtually none of this feedback during his 33 years with the company!*
>
> In fact, he continued, were it not for our coaching relationship, he probably would have abandoned some of the new behaviors he was trying because they seemed unappreciated and unimportant to the folks he wanted to affect. But, after hearing the feedback that evening, he recognized that his behavior changes *were* appreciated and important to the success of the business.

It was unfortunate that Mark did not hear more of that feedback when he needed it most: during the previous third of a century! We hear over and over again—that people are reluctant to give upward feedback—positive or constructive—and executives are often too proud to seek it.

Positive feedback needs to be timely to help others succeed. Imagine how much more powerful the feedback would have been if it had been delivered earlier! I wish this story were unique—but it is all too common that we hear executives share their frustration with receiving little feedback—especially positive feedback.

Key takeaways from this story:

- *Feedback* is vital to personal development and effectiveness.

- *Positive feedback* is rarely provided. Either we think people don't need it or we are uncomfortable providing it. And I've heard people say, "No one gives me feedback, so why should I bother providing it to someone else?" The truth is that each of us needs positive feedback—especially when learning a new behavior or making an effort to change old behaviors.

- *Specific feedback* on new and desired behaviors is rarely provided. If you provide positive, specific feedback for behaviors that matter in your business, we assure you it will have a significant impact on your people and your results.

Feedback takes time (for people who have little or none to spare). Feedback requires thought (by people racing from one task to the next). Feedback requires you to have knowledge—ideally, first-hand—of what the performer did (for leaders who travel more than they are in the office).

For these reasons, feedback gets put off the top-ten list and relegated to a when-I-have-time priority. **Don't let this happen to you!** Take charge and establish yourself as an encourager for things that matter to you and your business.

Why Don't We Give More Positive, Encouraging Feedback?

Here are common objections to using praise or positive feedback:

1. Our culture poorly teaches us how to give and receive positive feedback. We are often more comfortable using sarcasm or negativity.

2. Some believe we shouldn't be praised for performance that is "expected."

3. Individuals and teams need positive feedback at different intervals and detail levels. In general, we need frequent and detailed feedback when we are learning a new task or behavior. As we become more proficient, we need less-frequent, less-detailed feedback.

4. We often think that only our top performers deserve feedback. If we tell "mediocre" or average performers we are pleased with what they did, are we signaling that everything they do is OK? No, not if we pinpoint specifically the behaviors for which we are providing positive feedback.

POSITIVE FEEDBACK DELIVERY SKILLS

Delivering positive feedback well can be tricky. Not only must your delivery be effective, but you also must manage the receiver's reaction to your words. The following tips will help you give it with sincerity and confidence. We have separated them into "basic" and "advanced" techniques to signal progression toward excellence in feedback delivery.

Basic Techniques
(Must-Haves for Good Feedback Delivery)

1. Use the NORMS OF OBJECTIVITY to describe performance objectively, specifically, and sincerely. Rely on NORMS to help you specify behaviors you particularly value. Cite specific actions or events—what was the performance? How did you learn of it?

NORMS of Objectivity™

Not an Interpretation

Observable

Reliable

Measurable

Specific

2. Deliver feedback as soon as possible after the performance.
3. Don't wait until the performance is perfect. People need positive feedback when their performance improves. Provide feedback for small improvements in behavior. (We call this "shaping" performance—the next chapter covers the ins and outs of shaping.)
4. Make sure your feedback is **encouraging**. Observe whether performance improves or stays the same, and whether the person or team is more effective.

5. Don't say, "Great, but . . ." Don't mix positive and constructive feedback (which is feedback intended to change a behavior).

Advanced Techniques

1. Tell the person how you felt about the performance and the positive reactions you observed in others.

2. Talk about any other positive effects the performance might have on the team or others. (Describe how the person's actions create positive results for themselves, the team, or the organization.)

3. Get input from the person:
   - What did you seek to do?
   - How did you feel about what you did?
   - Has anyone else noticed?
   - Are you pleased with how this all came together?

Sincerity Is a Must

I take a hard line on sincerity. If you don't mean it—don't say it. You will compromise your own reputation as a leader to be trusted if you give insincere praise. Once you really grasp the behavioral power of your role as a leader/supervisor, you quickly understand how important your words of praise and support are to others.

Your feedback will be viewed as insincere if:

- *You know little about the person or the performance*

- *You make general statements like "great job" or "good work" or deliver an "aerosol spray" of positive feedback to everyone*

- *You don't allow time for questions or discussions*

- *You provide only positive feedback and never provide constructive feedback*

- *You provide feedback immediately after meeting the person*

- *You praise one person in front of others, with the goal of punishing those who haven't done the desired behavior.*

Create Winners!

Across time, try to deliver positive feedback four times for every instance of constructive feedback (4:1).

Precision Is Important

Let's look at some statements to contrast their effectiveness. Here are statements of expectation or feedback. Statements on the right have a greater impact on behavior than statements on the left. Can you see why?

Less Impact	Greater Impact
"Your customer satisfaction numbers are unacceptable."	"I want your western sales region to increase customer retention by at least 20% beyond current."
"The joint venture with Wystay Corp. has really worked out for us."	"As a result of our joint venture with Wystay, revenues and operating margins are up over 16%, utilization rates are 22% better, and both companies report increased earnings per share. I'm really pleased with our performance."
"Jerry is an inspirational leader."	"Several employees told me that when Jerry shared his vision, he excited folks and catalyzed their approach to group meetings."
"You own information technology for our company."	"I expect you to develop our IT strategy to align with our business strategy. You are accountable for the success of all IT purchases and implementations, except for our LAN/WAN."

Statements in the "Less Impact" column are vague and unspecific. Those in the "Greater Impact" column are more focused and identify specific behaviors or results.

Behavioral descriptions that relay specific expectations are more likely to prompt desired behaviors than the general descriptions in the "Less Impact" column. This is especially true in times of uncertainty or change, or when a performance is inconsistent with what is needed and behavior needs to change.

People can more easily change their behavior when they clearly understand the antecedents: specific expectations and communication of what is desired or needed.

Similarly, when consequences (like feedback) are precise and sincere, they have a stronger effect on behaviors they follow. Being told you did a "great job" has low impact. But suppose your boss is specific: "Your sales presentation to XYZ company was fantastic. It led to a $3.2M sale of our products over the next year. That puts us over the top for our revenue target for the quarter. Congratulations!"

When you hear that, it's hard not to feel good! Each of us, and leaders especially, has an amazing power to encourage desired behaviors—through our words, our attention, and our acts of support. Said behaviorally, by providing clear and necessary antecedents for the desired behaviors, and ensuring that the desired behaviors are encouraged by consequences, we can create an environment that enables each employee to be more successful. And if each of us performs well on strategically critical tasks, the company will perform well. Everyone wins!

Positive Feedback in Action—A Model

A client of ours, a freight transportation company, had embraced Behavioral Science company-wide. The company nominated "Ken"—a supervisor who embraced ABC analysis, pinpointing, and consequence analysis, driving them home to his reports—to receive an award for outstanding application of Behavioral Science daily on the job.

CLG consultant John Burden, who worked with Ken, quotes from the award nomination. It is a fine example of an organization using positive feedback to reward, encourage, and honor the desirable behavior of an employee—citing measurable results.

> Ken has been a role model during the implementation and integration of the behavioral approach into our operations. By setting clear expectations and encouraging productive behaviors, he has built a positive working relationship with

union employees, focusing on improving business results. His leadership has resulted in significant improvements:

- 2.75% increase—repair productivity
- 10% increase—inspection productivity
- 40% reduction—out-of-service downtime

Ken personalizes his contact with his employees and spends considerable time on the shop floor and in the field. This fosters an atmosphere where his employees can talk freely in their work environment.

As a result, Ken's employees give him continual feedback on ways to improve tasks and processes. His actions on their recommendations have been a critical component of employees' ability to deliver on productivity and safety targets.

His supervisor continually witnesses Ken in open discussions with his employees. He provides hands-on leadership by helping employees understand what is most important to the company's service delivery.

Ken is also a safety leader. He sets clear expectations in writing to his employees weekly in specific safety areas. He then personally audits and gives feedback and recognition to his employees, based on the weekly safety focus. Employees know exactly what they must do to prevent accidents, incidents, or injuries.

Ken also leads by example on worksites—for example, at accident sites—where he places strict adherence to safety procedures ahead of all else. As a result, he has cut reportable injuries by 50%. At this time, his employees have gone nearly half a year without a reportable injury.

Ken exemplifies the type of leader we demand. Among his peers, Ken is highly respected and demonstrates characteristics of a team player. He is willing to help any peer. We are proud to have him as a colleague, and feel that he should be recognized for his everyday contribution to our division and the company's success. Ken is truly deserving of recognition through the Award for Excellence for his work—and most importantly, the results.

CONSTRUCTIVE FEEDBACK IS NECESSARY FOR IMPROVEMENT

You might think that providing "all positive consequences" is best, but that is not so. People learn far faster and trust the feedback more when they receive a mixture of positive and constructive feedback. In the 4:1 ratio, the 1 (constructive feedback) is very important. Giving constructive feedback can be touchy . . . but remember, it is a gift.

> Those who really care about another's success will care enough to speak the truth—which means sharing suggestions for improvement. Give it as a gift, and receive it as such. It is vital to any person or group's growth and development.

Our distinction between *constructive feedback* and *negative feedback (criticism)* is deliberate. Negative feedback focuses on the "undesirable side" of performance and does little to help others improve. It simply points out the behaviors you no longer want. An unfortunate side effect of negative feedback is that it is often directed at the *person* rather than the *behavior*.

Constructive feedback, on the other hand, is more developmental in nature. It is intended *to discourage an undesired behavior and to clarify and encourage a preferred behavior*. Unlike criticism, which is intended to harmfully stop a behavior, constructive feedback works to replace the undesired behavior with a more effective behavior, and thus to decrease the likelihood that the undesired behavior will recur.

Constructive feedback has two components that operate together:

1. *Discouraging the undesired or less-effective behavior* by describing what was wrong with it and the negative impact it had.

2. *Specifying a preferred behavior* so you are sure the performer has knowledge of the desired behavior.

Constructive feedback is extremely effective when you recognize that you are replacing one behavior (undesired or less effective) with another behavior (preferred). For the new behavior (preferred) to really take hold, the performer must receive positive feedback about that behavior. This means that your job is to "catch the person doing it right" and to encourage his or her behavior by delivering sincere, positive feedback.

Remember, always pinpoint the undesirable behavior(s) as well as the desired behavior(s) when providing constructive feedback.

> **Use only . . .**
> NORMS-based observations and descriptors to provide good constructive feedback! Avoid subjective language. When giving feedback, be as pinpointed and NORMS-based as possible.

To illustrate effective use of constructive feedback, read this e-mail that one of our consultants received from Joseph, Operations Manager for a Fortune 100's specialty chemical plant:

> Here are my thoughts on Jane's coaching and feedback skills. There have been some pretty significant shifts in the past six months.
>
> Yesterday was my performance appraisal. Nothing she said surprised me. She has given me pretty regular feedback—at least twice per month—and she has direct access to what I do.
>
> She said my unit's productivity rate was 92%, below our stretch goal of 105%. But she congratulated me on the 92% and commented that I wouldn't have achieved that level if I weren't committed and working hard. We had a good discussion about why our unit didn't hit the stretch goal of 105%. Jane suggested that part of it was beyond my control due to the types of projects we are doing.
>
> The other part, maybe 7%, we agreed was within our control and could be improved. She shared observations of three instances where I did not follow through on commitments I had made. And she pointed out where my time could be more productively spent.

I felt really good about our discussion. As I said, it wasn't a surprise because we frequently discuss my performance, both good points and where I need help. She cited specific instances of how I've contributed to the work team.

For example, our team had completed 97% of my preventive maintenance tasks. I'd forgotten some of that stuff and was amazed that she knew it.

Another thing Jane did, which made me feel great, was pass along compliments others have made about my work. It was important to her that I knew how others felt.

What else can I say? It's 180 degrees from where we were a year ago, and it's made all the difference for our unit. Thanks for your role in helping Jane make the transition. I know she trusts you a great deal, and I can see why.

—Joseph

What is it about Jane's feedback that makes Joseph feel good about his accomplishments and areas for growth? You can see that Jane provides NORMS-based feedback about behaviors within Joseph's control, and she provides frequent feedback about behaviors, not just results. She also suggests specific behaviors to change to increase productivity. *Feedback can act as both a consequence (by increasing or decreasing the likelihood of behavior in the future) and an antecedent (as information that guides future behavior).*

Let's take a detailed look at Jane's behavior and its consequences for Joseph's behavior.

Antecedents	Behavior	Consequences	Consequence Analysis			
			EFFECT on behavior (Encourage, Discourage)	TIMING (Immediate, Delayed)	IMPOR-TANCE to performer (High, Low)	PROBA-BILITY (Likely, Unlikely)
Jane's deliberate observations of Joseph's performance	Jane provided specific descriptions of performance (some with measures)	Joseph felt good about his accomplish-ments	Encourage	Immediate	High	Likely
Jane spent time in operations and observed behavior	Jane had frequent performance discussions with Joseph	Joseph knew how she felt about his performance	Encourage or Discourage	Immediate	High	Likely
Jane's pinpoints, based on her observations of Joseph's performance and her technical expertise	Jane provided specific examples of how performance can be improved	Joseph has a better understanding of how he can spend his time	Encourage	Immediate	High	Likely

Joseph is not left wondering what he should be doing, or what behaviors are valued by his supervisor and others.

CONSTRUCTIVE FEEDBACK DELIVERY SKILLS

Since constructive feedback can be especially challenging, use the following important tips to deliver effective, constructive feedback. Again, these tips are divided into two levels, basic and advanced.

Basic Techniques
(Must-Haves for Good Feedback Delivery)

First, evaluate:

- Whether you've clearly stated your expectations *(antecedents)* and provided direction on how to meet the goal or performance expectations
- Whether you have provided the proper tools for the person to perform the expected task
- Whether you have given timely, relevant performance feedback
- Whether you have praised the person for making progress toward the goal *(consequence)*

If you haven't done these first, don't try to correct the other person's performance by providing constructive feedback. Rather, correct your *own* performance, as you have not given the person what he or she needs to be successful!

If you have clearly stated your expectations, provided direction and tools, and given feedback and praise for improvements in performance, use the following techniques for providing constructive feedback:

1. Discuss the performance privately.
2. Don't provide constructive feedback when you are angry (unless behavior is life-threatening).
3. Talk to the performer as soon as possible after the performance occurs—do not store up or postpone feedback.
4. Be specific and objective when discussing undesired performance. Use the **NORMS OF OBJECTIVITY** when describing the behavior. What was the performance? When and where

did it occur? How did you come to know about the performance?

5. Describe the desired performance specifically. Again, use the **NORMS OF OBJECTIVITY** to describe what you would prefer to see the person do.

6. Talk about behavior, not the individual's personality traits.

7. Catch the person doing it right. Look for opportunities to encourage behavior change and improvement.

8. Remember that when it's over, it's over. Don't punish the person. Focus on the behavior and support evidence of desired behaviors.

9. Use "I" statements—own your message. Rather than saying, "*You* need to improve," try saying, "*I'd* like to see you try . . ."

More Advanced Techniques

1. Give the feedback in a climate of trust and support.

2. Describe to the person the consequences of undesired performance for you, others, the team, and the organization.

3. Describe how you felt about the performance.

4. Get the person to participate and talk.

5. Get the person to agree that a problem exists.

6. Get the person to offer solutions.

7. Agree on one solution and have the person summarize your discussion.

Create Winners!

Provide constructive feedback even though it might be uncomfortable for you. People need to know when they are not performing as they should be/need to be—and you can help them win by helping them to be better. Remember: feedback is a gift we can all give—thoughtfully and well.

**Most of Us Avoid Accepting
Constructive Feedback. Why?**

- *It is often difficult to own our personal developmental needs. And it is even more difficult to acknowledge your needs in the presence of another person.*

- *We are concerned about potential negative consequences for acknowledging a weakness or developmental need.*

- *Dealing with a developmental need forces us to examine an aspect of our behavior that we may be aware of but prefer to avoid discussing.*

- *We think that our situation is unique and cannot be understood by anyone else.*

- *It is often phrased in a blaming manner instead of in a concerned, suggesting way, making us angry with the deliverer of the feedback.*

- *Many of us have consequence histories that suggest bad things will happen to us if we acknowledge an improvement area.*

In general, it comes down to more subjective and person-specific things such as pride, self-evaluation, and desire for success. This is why effective delivery of feedback can be tricky to do well.

SHARING FEEDBACK: THE FINE ART OF COACHING

Feedback is an essential part of applying Behavioral Science, but the "how" of delivering feedback is a fine art. We deliver feedback through coaching.

By now you should have a good feel for feedback—what it is and why it is important. Your next question is probably, "How do I bring feedback to life?"

Feedback Comes to Life Through Coaching

Each of us has a consequence history with coaching, so coaching means something slightly different to each of us. For us, coaching is a "caring sharing" of feedback in a relationship of mutual trust and respect. Coaching integrates all the NORMS-based data to help the recipient attain better performance. To bring coaching to life, we will share our coaching model with you.

Coaching has three steps: *observing, analyzing performance, and delivering feedback to shape performance.* Whether we are coaching you, or you are coaching a direct report, all three steps apply.

1. *Observing.* Gathering NORMS-based data on performance begins with observation. This step involves observing behavior or reviewing written products to understand the effects of the person's behavior on others. The objective is to sample first-hand the individual's behavior.

In an ideal world, we would watch videotape of a person's behavior so we could replay the parts we and they most care about. But that's unrealistic. Instead, we do non-intrusive direct observation and take notes on what the person says or does. (This builds a valuable database of specific examples to which we can refer when we deliver our feedback.) We also speak with others who directly sample a person's behavior, so we can obtain additional (and often historical) examples.

2. *Analyzing Performance.* From your observations, pinpoint specific behaviors and the context in which they occur. Analyze why the behaviors occur. See what antecedents are prompting them—and what consequences are encouraging them. Especially look to see if the person is receiving sufficient encouragement for desired behaviors.

3. *Delivering Feedback to Shape Performance.* This is where one-on-one feedback, both positive and constructive, is shared. (This also can be done with a team.) During the coaching discussion, several things should occur:

- Specifically identify the performances, either desired or less preferred (this is done either by you or by the person receiving the coaching).

- Communicate your specific observations along with your qualitative impressions about the behaviors you observed.

- Make certain the individual is clear about what they're doing that's on target, and what they need to do differently.

- Encourage the individual to problem-solve how to encourage and sustain a new, desired behavior.

In actual coaching, these steps recur, sometimes fairly seamlessly and rapidly. A good coach maintains a 4:1 ratio of positive to constructive feedback over time. The individual receiving the feedback should know you care and are trying to help him or her. That requires sincerity in how you give the feedback and in the words you choose.

Coaching, Feedback, and the Labor Shortage

In today's competitive market for good employees, coaching is an extraordinarily valuable tool for retaining your people. Individuals want to feel valued; they want to make a difference. People have more choices today than ever before as to where they work and what they do. Individuals are choosing to stay with companies where they see growth and development opportunities. People want to know what's *in it* for them, not just what's *expected of* them.

Companies with feedback-rich environments help people feel valued and appreciated. People choose to be there and give their discretionary performance freely. Organizations with little or no feedback or one-way feedback tend to have higher turnover, lower overall morale, and more *compliant* behaviors than *commitment* behaviors (or discretionary performance).

Here is a quick test of whether feedback and coaching can be a power tool in your company's culture:

1. If your company uses an employee commitment survey, are the lowest scores in provision of feedback, listening to employees, or discussing career development plans?

2. Do you often hear people complain, "I'm not sure what's expected of me?" or "I don't know what they think about my performance?"

3. Do supervisors resist completing performance reviews?

If the answer is "yes" to any of these questions, your organization most likely needs more feedback and coaching.

EXECUTIVE COACHING

We see increasing use of executive coaches. And rightly so, for it is a tremendous value-add, leading to a better bottom line:

1. *Sustained levels of high performance within organizations begin with the effectiveness of executive leadership.* Executive leaders need to establish an environment where people understand business priorities and values, have the necessary resources to perform, and most importantly, want to perform at high levels. Their performance is critical to the success of the organization.

2. *Executives rarely get feedback.* Most organizations today are a hotbed of politics. Evaluation of an executive's behavior may not be well received—particularly if the evaluation is unsolicited. Thus, the use of an outside coach provides a safe haven where executives get feedback, talk about their own insecurities and needs, and have available an objective, caring resource whose main concern is the executive's success—unencumbered by any personal agenda an insider might have.

3. *The tenure of an executive has never been shorter or more performance-dependent.* Executives have no room to deliver below expectations. Combine this with the typical dearth of feedback, and you have a potentially combustible combination. The use of an outside coach cuts the cycle time of feedback from the critical players—if delivered by an effective behavioral coach. Even the world's best athletes have coaches.

Seek and Ye Shall Find

Leaders have power, and this, combined with their formal positions, often isolates them from honest feedback, even if they report being comfortable receiving feedback. The truth is, many people have grown up in organizations where they tell leaders what they think the leaders want to hear. They have seen these behaviors heavily encouraged within their organizations.

Don't let this be you! Feedback is critical to your own growth and development, and it's necessary for you to understand the environment accurately enough to make good business decisions. Successful leaders seek constructive feedback and realize it is necessary for their personal development and their organization's development.

TAKEAWAYS ON FEEDBACK AND COACHING

Here are the key points to take from this chapter:

1. *Feedback is one of the most powerful consequences for behavior.* Feedback is most powerful when it is Encouraging, follows behavior Immediately, is of High Importance to the performer, and is Likely to occur. Providing feedback about behaviors that create business results is the secret of some of the best leaders I've known.

2. *There are three types of feedback for your leadership toolbox:*

   - **Positive feedback** is used to encourage desired behaviors. When delivered effectively, positive feedback also leaves a person feeling great about his or her accomplishments.

   - **Constructive feedback** is used to discourage less-desired behaviors and replace them with preferred behaviors. When delivered effectively, constructive feedback helps individuals understand how to be more successful while making them feel good about their accomplishments so far.

   - **No feedback**—the absence of feedback also affects behavior. And it affects attitudes and morale. When a desired behavior is not followed by feedback, it may decrease. When a less-preferred behavior is not followed by feedback, it is likely to continue. The point is that providing no feedback leaves behaviors—and business results—to chance. Don't take that risk.

   In the next chapter, we will explore the important process of shaping behavior. Shaping is about encouraging behaviors through the use of feedback, a key step in achieving a desired behavior goal. Shaping is an important skill for leaders—it's about helping people grow and develop.

Highlighting Excellence . . .

Priceless Coaching at AEO

An interview with Tom DiDonato, Executive Vice President of Human Resources, American Eagle Outfitters

"**A** clothing store that appeals to the 15-to-25-year-old shopper has to be on its toes. You need to be consistently on-trend, offering compelling merchandise with an important value component. We are, I am proud to say, very successful at attracting these shoppers. With more than 900 stores and 20,000 employees, we finished 2006 with $2.8 billion in sales.

But it wasn't always this way! Like a lot of great companies, we struggled. For example, 2003 was a non-bonus year. We weren't hitting on all cylinders.

In 2004, we surveyed employees: "What isn't working?" They told us: "We don't feel empowered. We feel micromanaged. We aren't recognized. We don't understand our roles and responsibilities. We're not being developed. We work in silos, with little cross-functionality. We don't know where we are going." The company needed a distinctive culture and workplace, and these survey results were not good.

Our executives blamed themselves: "We have to be doing something wrong. We want to change—and fast—because we don't have much time if we want to retain our best people." Our senior managers felt lost; they didn't know what was going on. In 2004, our senior directors felt disenfranchised. Some of our leaders didn't even seem to know the mission! These were key people, with a lot of associates reporting to them.

So every leader went through a 360° assessment, and committed to a coach for nine months. The leaders and coaches developed action items that the leaders needed to drive, because all change starts from the top.

I have always been somewhat cynical about the effectiveness of coaching. Coaching can be like a massage—you feel good at the time, but there is nothing sustainable.

But this was not soft coaching. It involved helping leaders actually solve business problems the right way. How do you include people? How do you empower people? The coach "checked in" with the direct reports for feedback over the course of the coaching experience to understand if improvements were being seen; action plans were adjusted as necessary.

Our senior directors got on board. When you get management this engaged and this positive, good things happen.

Then we did a resurvey, asking "How are we doing?" The results were very encouraging. That is why we are winning now. The last three years have been unbelievable. We have had double-target years! We are exceeding Wall Street's expectations. Our team is firing on all cylinders.

We know where we are going, we are focused on strategy and achieving our goals, so the micromanaging has dissipated. Cross-functional meetings are now commonplace. We have so many recognition forums that we have taken advantage of, and it makes a big difference. Executives are part of a team, and all executives roll up their sleeves and get their hands dirty. So the coaching is very positive.

Now, people get the short-term and long-term goals. They know our strategy. People are always encouraged to think outside the box, but since they know the vision and understand our strategy, ideas now drive our business consistent with our well-developed strategy.

On the value of coaches . . .

First—we learned a lot. Coaches have played a critical role in helping us elevate our culture. But coaches aren't created equal. One learning is to make sure you really match the coach with the situation you are trying to address.

Second—coaches do not replace open and candid feedback. Leaders must own communication and feedback. You have to be good at delivering feedback, and it has to come personally.

Third—coaches must have goals, and their effectiveness needs to be measured. Look for sustainable change and focus on key areas. Our coaches focused on helping leaders solve business problems using practical approaches.

How much is a coach worth? If you do those three things right, a coach is priceless."

Shaping Up the Right Stuff

"Of all the behavioral tools I've learned, 'shaping' most caused me to question my approach to leadership. When I saw its emphasis on encouraging progress toward a desired goal, I realized that I was probably being too hard on my people. I have very high standards. I know that, and am often told that by others. I am also quick to point out what is wrong about a situation or how far we still need to go. (I am an engineer, and that continuous-improvement blood flows through this mind and body at all times!)

"I was much less skilled at pointing out what was positive—and where progress had been made. I had probably kept morale lower—and perhaps, even hurt individuals' progress—by not helping them see all the good they had done and the progress they had made.

"Now, I could not be more different. Without lowering my standards, I have developed a purposeful approach to recognizing and encouraging progress—and I do it with rigor and reliability. I hate to admit, but I have to say that I feel better, too. I feel happier—and it is clear, my people feel more prideful about their work and excited to keep getting better—without my needing to suggest it. Shaping was key to engaging my people in a whole different way."

—*International Division President,*
Fortune 30 Company

HOW DO WE get good at what we do? Excellent behavior doesn't happen overnight. Think back to when you learned how to do something new. Did you learn to ski well overnight? Did you ace your serve the first time you played tennis? Were you a great speaker the first time you had to talk in front of a large group?

So, how do we learn complex, advanced behaviors? Conventional wisdom tells us that "practice makes perfect." But we all know that isn't necessarily the case. If you grip your tennis racket incorrectly and bend your wrist while hitting the ball, all the practice in the world won't help your game. So sometimes we say, "*perfect* practice makes perfect." But that really isn't the case, either.

Behavioral Science tells us that practice—even perfect practice—is not the main ingredient for developing behaviors. The recipe is a process called **shaping**. Its ingredients are *behavior, feedback,* and *increasingly challenging behavioral goals.*

Here is a shaping story . . .

Randy is an engaging and energetic public speaker. He makes eye contact with everyone, smiles, rarely relies on notes, and uses humor at appropriate points. After watching Randy deliver a presentation at a company conference, I complimented him. He smiled shyly. "You know, it took me a long time to become this comfortable in front of a large group of people." He shared his story . . .

> **I started my career in technology. My job was to interface with our customers and understand their issues with our products. I had a wonderful supervisor, Karl. We used to have long talks about issues in our department and how to address them.**
>
> **One day Karl asked me to organize my thoughts and present them at a staff meeting. I was terrified! There were only five people in the meeting, but it felt like 500! I scripted my presentation and read it word-for-word as fast as I could. I don't think I even looked up from my paper.**

Soon after, Karl complimented me on my presentation. Then, in a very caring way, he asked why I was so nervous.

We had a great talk. He thought my ideas were great, and went precisely in the right direction for our department. In fact, he suggested I could play a major leadership role in helping us get there. But it would require me to become more comfortable with public speaking and communicating to groups. So, I began my journey, with Karl's help.

Our technology and product sales folks gather annually for a two-day conference. Karl and I set my goal: to give a short presentation to about 50 people at one meeting. I had three months to prepare. He said my content was on target and didn't need much coaching.

I would focus on three areas: use of notes, eye contact, and voice projection. We also looked for relatively safe opportunities for me to speak, like weekly staff meetings, customer calls, etc.

It wasn't easy, but with Karl's help, I made a lot of progress. I went from scripting and reading my presentation, to putting key points in large type on paper, to using slides with note cards. Karl was often there to provide feedback.

I'll never forget the meeting when I looked up and saw my coworkers smiling. What a rush! I felt they were really on my side. A little later, I took a risk and told a joke. People laughed! I couldn't believe it. I started to get hooked. People were actually listening and appreciating what I said.

Well, I gave my presentation at that yearly conference. I couldn't eat for two days before it. But I did well. My goal was to use slides and only look at my note cards if I absolutely needed to. In fact, I only brought two note cards.

After my presentation, Karl went wild—he was so proud of me. And the head nods throughout my talk were reinforcing as well. Since then, I've really worked on my presentation skills. I've learned to identify an area to work on, and then take it slow. I've used coaches to give me feedback. And I always look at the audience to see if I'm getting a positive reaction to what I'm doing. It's made all the difference in the world.

Clearly, Randy was not a born public speaker. He had to *shape* his presentation skills. No wonder he is now such an effective speaker! He applied shaping and worked on his skills over time. Here are some things Randy did:

- *Bits and Pieces.* He broke the complex behavior of speaking at the conference into "behavioral chunks," or bite-sized pieces he could work on. He focused on his use of notes, eye contact, and voice projection.

- *Just Within Reach.* Randy set a goal for himself—to give his presentation using only slides. That was a stretch, considering his starting point was reading from a script. But he didn't make the mistake of leaping toward his goal all at once. He set small, attainable sub-goals toward which to work. He put key points on paper in very large type that he could see easily, so he could turn back to his audience. Later, he started to use slides with note cards. Eventually, he used fewer note cards and referenced them less.

- *Practice and Feedback.* Randy and Karl identified plenty of practice opportunities. Randy received feedback during and after every opportunity. He saw people smiling and nodding—a natural consequence of making eye contact with the audience. He also experienced a very powerful natural consequence when people laughed at his joke. In addition to natural consequences, Randy received social consequences from Karl in the form of feedback. And Randy gave himself feedback on his performance.

- *Upping the Ante.* Randy kept pushing himself. Once he reached a goal, he raised the bar a little more and found ways to get feedback about his performance.

THE SCIENCE OF SHAPING

> **Shaping . . .**
>
> is a process . . .
> of differentially encouraging . . .
> successive approximations of behavior toward a goal.

Shaping is both science and art. The science lies in using proven Behavioral Science techniques to isolate and encourage the right behaviors. The art lies in knowing when and how to apply those techniques. Let us take an everyday example to further understand the science of shaping.

Shaping Behavior from Current to Desired

We said that "shaping is a process of differentially encouraging successive approximations of behavior toward a goal." But what does this scientific definition really mean? Let's examine its three pieces:

- *Shaping is a process* . . . a set of steps that get you from where you are to where you want to be. Shaping steps develop a behavior from its *current* state to a *desired state*.

- *Shaping is a process of differentially encouraging* . . . the performer must receive encouragement for a behavior. And the performer must *not* receive encouragement for *other* behaviors. "Differential encouragement" means that behaviors are clearly distinguished from one another— some to be encouraged and others not.

- *Shaping is a process of differentially encouraging successive approximations of behavior toward a goal.* Behaviors are differentiated by how close they are to the final behavioral goal.

Shaping behavior is about perfecting a **chain of behavioral steps** *through the systematic application of encouragement.* To progress up the behavioral chain, behaviors closer to the goal need to be more encouraging than earlier behaviors.

Providing encouragement for behaviors earlier in the chain will only sustain those behaviors, which are just steppingstones toward the goal. But we don't want those behaviors sustained in isolation; we want to promote the *next* behavior in the chain.

Shaping on the Internet

The Internet is another great example of shaping in action, with all the powerfully encouraging aspects of information right at your fingertips. The Internet offers easy access to product visualization and ordering, visual and auditory prompts that cue your next click, etc.

In fact, in the past decade, technology developers have demonstrated a striking awareness of how to shape human behavior. Their programs guide us very effectively toward certain outcomes and purchasing behaviors—behaviors that otherwise would not occur.

The next time you are online, study the websites and links. Note how they smoothly prompt you along—powerfully shaping you all the way!

Remember that size of the steps matters:

- If the shaping steps are *too big* (like ordering a product online when you've not used a computer before), the behavior will cease mid-chain.

- If the shaping steps are *too small* (like clicking on links that lead only to more lists of links, which lead to more links, taking forever to reach the information you seek), the behavior will cease mid-chain due to the delay or absence of encouraging consequences for those additional "clicks." Careful sequencing and provision of encouragement for new behaviors is critical for shaping to work.

THE ART OF SHAPING

Shaping is a scientific process, but has a strong artistic side. Let's look at the art of shaping—applying your behavioral skills. As with any process, shaping requires that you start with an end in mind. *What is the behavior you ultimately want?* This is where you call upon your pinpointing skills. Start by identifying key behaviors that lead to results.

Once your goal is clear, examine where the performers are right now. *What current behaviors could be shaped toward the desired end state?* Use what you've learned about ABCs to pinpoint current behaviors.

Example: Improving General Managers' Budgets, Profit Forecasts

The goal: *General Managers submit more accurate budgets and operating profit forecasts.*

The current behavior (not good):

- GMs are routinely late in submitting budgets and profit plans.

- GMs submit budgets that do not include all planned costs from product specialists at the plants.

- GMs submit profit targets that do not align with those of Sales and are generally not within 10% of actuals.

- Management often does not understand or follow budgets and forecasts.

- GMs submit funding requests for additional projects that arrive after budgets are approved. Although not included in original budgets, they appear to be legitimate.

What shaping steps are needed? You know where you want to go (desired behavior) and where you will begin (current behavior), so you need a path—a chain of steps—for getting from here to there. What behavioral steps can the performers take to get where you want them to be?

Shaping Step 1	Communicate the business case. In this instance, it's the need to improve budget adherence and operating profit through forecasting accuracy.
Shaping Step 2	Communicate the goal of getting budgets/profit plans submitted on time, improving cash flow through lower inventory levels, and increasing accuracy through communication among key groups. Encourage these behaviors when they occur.
Shaping Step 3	Hold meetings for finance staff members, general managers, business managers, sales managers, product specialists, and plant staff. Share information and update forecasts. Praise (encourage) attendance at the meetings and information-sharing when these behaviors occur.
Shaping Step 4	Have GMs conduct a comparative review with the Divisional VP to ensure accuracy of numbers across the different reporting groups. Praise (encourage) behaviors that lead to accuracy of numbers.
Shaping Step 5	Have GMs understand the fluctuations between expected and actual monthly financial results and the business plan commitment. Engage the original group (GMs, business managers, sales managers, and product specialists) in identifying root causes of inaccurate or inconsistent data. Develop process or behavioral change plans to prevent future occurrences.
Shaping Step 6	Implement the corrective actions and align information-sharing to improve accuracy of financial reports. Ensure that contributions are recognized and encouraged.
Shaping Step 7	Monitor progress and communicate the trend data regarding actuals and forecasts to ensure that all parties recognize their roles and contributions to the measured improvements.
Shaping Step 8	Track the percentage reduction and the gap between expected and actual financial results. Encourage contributors if the data trend in the right direction.
Shaping Step 9	Incorporate the new learnings into revised work processes, training, communication, etc. so they become a regular part of how forecasts and budgets are determined.
Shaping Step 10	Use a discretionary recognition/reward process for participants who help achieve improved outcomes. Give written praise so you can discuss it during performance review. Encourage team members to praise one another for progress.

Size of Behavioral Steps Matters

It is important to identify accurately the size of the behavioral steps. This is one of the trickiest parts, and most crucial, of the shaping process. If you make behavioral steps too big, performers are less likely to succeed. Most people find that failing to reach a goal is very punishing, so they quit trying.

Here are examples—

Behavioral Step Too Big—Remember Randy's public speaking dilemma? If his boss, Karl, had tried to encourage Randy to go immediately from reading his scripted notes word-for-word to presenting with slides and no notes, Randy probably would have failed, too frustrated to try again.

Behavioral Step Too Small—The flip side is making behavioral steps too small. Imagine creating so many sub-steps for behavior that you have trouble telling how much progress you really make from one step to the next, and maybe even forget where you are in the process.

Behavioral Step Just Right—When behavioral steps are just right, they are both challenging and realistic:

- *Challenging.* When people first try a new behavioral step, it should feel a little uncomfortable. They should feel like they need practice at the behavior.

- *Realistic.* While the behavioral steps should be challenging, they also must be realistic. The performer should be able to do the behavior on the first try, if awkwardly. This way, the performer receives some encouraging consequences for the behavior. If the performer tries the behavior and fails, he or she takes a step backward.

A LEADER'S ROLE IN SHAPING

When we talk shaping with leaders, we commonly hear, "It makes sense; the process sounds straightforward; I see how it can work. But I don't have *time* to manage antecedents and consequences that systematically!"

On one hand, these leaders are correct. Their busy schedules afford little extra time. On the other hand, they have far more opportunities available for shaping than they realize! Here is an example from a recent conversation with a client:

> PAUL *(THE CLIENT):* I think I understand the shaping process. I want to try it. But honestly, Hilary, I don't have the time!

> HILARY: Paul, you can *leverage the time you already have booked.* For example, you will see the GMs next week at the quarterly reviews. Why not use that as an opportunity for shaping their behavior?

> PAUL: OK . . . but what would I do?

> HILARY: Start by looking at the behavioral pinpoints you have for each GM. Look at the data you have about their behavior. You have some information, but you probably need more to have a meaningful conversation about their performance. Right?

> PAUL: Absolutely. Take Hal for example. My shaping target for him is this: get him to identify *honestly* the factors contributing to his making/not making his numbers. I feel like I'm getting a snow job about his division's operating performance. I learn about incidents long after the fact—generally from one of Hal's direct reports—and I rarely get the full story on the root causes . . .

> . . . In our last quarterly review, I saw numbers indicating we were going to make only 82% of our target for the quarter, due to "unforeseen changes in the market." That's not good enough for me—especially when our other divisions are affected by the same market conditions and are making 100% or greater of their target. Plus, an 18% deficit should not come to my attention for the first time in quarterly reviews!

Notice that Paul just gave our consultant information about several behavioral pinpoints for Hal that would directly impact business results: (1) giving Paul advance knowledge of the operating performance of Hal's division (especially when it is below forecast), (2) sharing a root-cause analysis of incidents that occurred within his division (including their effect on operating performance), and (3) detailing what factors impacted divisional performance, including marketplace changes, etc.

HILARY: OK. That tells me you need to know more about the general performance of Hal's division, outside the quarterly reviews as well as within them. Now that we've identified the desired behaviors, let's see if we have the proper antecedents to prompt them and the consequences to encourage progress toward them.

Note that our consultant encouraged Paul to consider the current antecedents and consequences to ensure they wouldn't encourage undesired behaviors or unintentionally prevent the desired behaviors he was looking for.

PAUL: Great. See this three-page memo? It details what I expect in the quarterly meetings. These are the antecedents, which I send one month before reviews, to each GM. See where I ask them to explain deviations and root-cause analysis on incidents?

HILARY: Hmm, looks pretty thorough. Let's talk about past reviews, because *consequence histories* are powerful antecedents. What happened in past quarterly reviews when Hal failed to share the information you requested?

PAUL: Well—nothing, I guess. I mean, I'll ask him where it is, but he glosses over the whole thing. To avoid getting behind, I usually let it go and move on to the next GM's report. It's a lot more rewarding for me to hear from my other GMs, because they *do* give me the information I need.

HILARY: Well, we might have just identified a powerful consequence that is maintaining the very behavior you DON'T want! Sounds like Hal gets encouraged for the way in which he provides his data. See it from his viewpoint: he gets to sit down quicker, doesn't have to explain why he didn't make his numbers, etc. The absence of any constructive feedback from you just encourages his old behaviors, the very ones you want to change. Hal knows he might receive constructive feedback he doesn't want to hear, if he details the problems he finds.

It is always important to examine the consequences that may be sustaining current behaviors—especially if they are behaviors you wish to shape toward new or different ones. As mentioned, the current behavior is NOT to be encouraged, while a newer behavior IS to be encouraged.

HILARY: Let's detail the behaviors you need from Hal, ones you can support through encouragement.

PAUL: I guess I'd begin by asking detailed questions about his division's performance. Then I'd say that I need such information in his formal quarterly review reports. I also could ask him to review why they made their numbers, or didn't—and be sure not to jump down his throat, even if I think he screwed up. I should encourage his telling me—and calmly work through the content of what happened at a different time. Does that sound about right?

Note that Paul picked up on the fact that he needs to withhold any negativity—despite the frustration he knows he will feel! The behavior of Hal's sharing openly and honestly will be fragile at first, and needs to be encouraged. The content of his message should be handled separately, so that Hal does not feel Paul is "shooting the messenger."

HILARY: Yes, that sounds right. Also, I recommend that we look at your calendar for the next 60 days to identify other times when you will have contact with Hal, so you can encourage the behaviors we've pinpointed. We can evaluate whether you have enough opportunities to shape the behaviors you need from Hal, or if you need to add shaping time into your calendar. We can repeat this process for the other GMs as well.

Note that we are arranging a system that allows Paul to keep in touch with the progress his folks are making on strategically critical areas. He will be able to reinforce or shape evidence of desired behaviors if he is seeking opportunities to do so.

PAUL: Sounds good. Here's my calendar . . .

When we have these conversations with leaders, our goal is to emphasize three key points:

1. *Every interaction you have with performers is a shaping opportunity.* Look at the time booked on your calendar and ask how you can leverage that time to shape behaviors that matter to the business.

2. *You need to gather information to maximize your shaping effectiveness.* You probably don't know enough about the performers' behaviors, or the results they are producing, to provide specific and meaningful feed-

back. One of the best ways to gather this data is to talk to those who have access to the performers' behaviors and results.

3. ***You need to develop a plan for shaping behavior.***
It's not enough to look at your calendar. You have to organize the information: Who are the performers? What are the shaping targets? When will you see the performers next? What information do you need to provide feedback?

You can use a simple table to organize this information. I call it a *Shaping Opportunity Grid*. For each event on your calendar, map out the following:

Shaping Opportunity Grid

Target Audience	Opportunity	Purpose	Plan and Approach
Who will be influenced through the contact?	*Events available for use as shaping opportunities*	*Business objectives, focus of encouragement*	*Actions to take, things to look for, how I will get information prior to contact*
Hal	Quarterly review meetings Weekly phone conferences Lunch next week	Encourage honest reporting of factors that contribute to his division making its numbers Encourage advance reporting of operating performance Encourage sharing of root-cause analyses of incidents	Prior to quarterly review, ask Hal for a preview of his report. Clarify what I'm looking for during review Ask Hal problem-solving questions about problem areas Encourage Hal's sharing of information, even if bad news

Then you need to ask, "Who performs behaviors that are critical to the success and profitability of the organization, but is NOT on my calendar?" Can you access that person's behaviors (and thus provide encouragement) via phone conversations, e-mail, or voicemail? In our company, the *Shaping Opportunity Grid* has become a standard part of our Executive Coaching technique.

The typical leader becomes boxed into certain patterns of action, based on what people *think* he/she wants to hear or see. Generally, the result is a dog-and-pony show that takes weeks of preparation by the field people (time taken from work they *should* be doing).

You can halt this dog-and-pony routine by working through the *Shaping Opportunity Grid*. The results? Your employees will actually *know* what you want to hear and see, so they will use their time better. And you can use the grid to prompt yourself, to think through how you can reinforce their desired behaviors. Together, you'll be able to shape the organization's progress toward aggressive, strategic, and profitable performance.

TAKEAWAYS ON SHAPING

Shaping is critical because it pulls together Behavioral Science theory into a practical application: influencing behavior. Shaping is about pinpointing desired behaviors—those that lead to business results—and then applying antecedents and consequences to build up those desired behaviors. Here are key points to remember about shaping:

1. *Shaping is "the process of differentially encouraging successive approximations of behavior toward a goal."* Shaping behavior is about perfecting a chain of behavioral steps by systematically applying encouragement toward a desired end. To progress up the behavioral chain, behaviors closer to the goal need to be more strongly encouraged than earlier behaviors. Providing encouragement for behaviors earlier in the chain will only sustain them, and they are just steppingstones toward the goal.

2. *The first step in shaping is to carefully pinpoint the desired behavior and discuss it with the performer.* Use your pinpointing skills to identify a behavior that drives important results. (Some might feel manipulated to learn a shap-

ing plan is operating on them, so it is always best to do it "with them," not "to them.")

3. *Use your pinpointing skills to identify the behavioral steps between the current behavior and the desired behavior.* Remember, the size of those behavioral steps must be both challenging and realistic. If too big, the performer is unlikely to meet the goals. If too small, the performer is likely to become bored or frustrated.

4. *Use ABC analysis to identify the antecedents and consequences required to influence the selected behaviors.*

5. *Use your feedback and coaching skills to see every interaction as a shaping opportunity.* Feedback and coaching are the primary tools for shaping behaviors.

6. *Rely on the Shaping Opportunity Grid* to help you organize your feedback and increase the likelihood that you will successfully shape behavior.

AN IMPORTANT MILESTONE IN YOUR JOURNEY

You now have the tools to effectively influence behavior for business results. You have a new perspective on why some organizations so effectively execute strategies, implement change, and maneuver in the marketplace when others cannot.

In the next chapter, our focus shifts from individual performance to organizational performance. We'll discuss business execution from a behavioral perspective. You will see yourself and others in the true business stories.

Each of us becomes part of a "change effort" at some point—whether leading it or being influenced by it. You will learn to apply the principles and tools in this book to avoid the many traps on your way to "Making Change Happen—Consistently and Well."

Highlighting Excellence . . .

Shaping Performance Over Time

The senior management of a major international oil company was dissatisfied with the performance of its Sub-Saharan Africa refinery in safety, environmental exceedances, reliability, and utilization. The site was considered the most challenging refinery in the system.

There were ongoing shutdown and startup problems, workplace injuries, and environmental incidents. Long lists of actions generated by audits were incomplete, and turnover among skilled workers was high.

All of this led to an unacceptable safety record, lost profitability, and poor community relations. Something had to change.

Paul, a recently appointed Refinery General Manager, was tasked to help turn the refinery around. In addition to the host of issues that the audit team had already uncovered, he quickly learned that the unionized workers considered management "the enemy." Refinery employees and contractors routinely strode through the facility without hard hats, safety glasses, or other protective gear—they knew the rules; they just neglected to follow them.

Paul was told, "We have to remember that many of our people live in communities with a high crime rate. You can't expect people to wear personal protective equipment and think about safety at work when they're worried about being shot at home."

His management team conducted a "back to basics" campaign and started to address the conditions that had eroded labor-management trust over the years. They stressed the importance of getting the fundamentals right the first time. They also researched benchmarks that defined world-class performance, and identified refinery-level gaps.

"It was a start," Paul recalls, but it still wasn't enough. "After six months, safety hadn't improved, and environmental exceedances were worse. We'd suffered a refinery-wide shutdown and a serious fire."

Paul's team had begun to change attitudes, but had failed to change performance.

So he contacted CLG, which assigned consultant Annemarie Michaud to help Paul formulate a plan to improve four results targets: safety, environmental concerns, incident reduction, and lost profit opportunity. They would proactively apply behavior-based leadership.

Managers, engineers, and first-line supervisors were introduced to Performance-Based Leadership™ (PBL). Coaching action plans were developed with each refinery leader, aligned with the four result areas. Three internal coaches supported the facility's 85 managers and supervisors, with distance support by CLG. Anecdotal progress, behavior change results, and leading/lagging business metrics were monitored monthly by the leadership team to ensure results were being achieved.

In addition, the refinery made several work process changes to better align responsibilities with business metrics. They introduced diagonal cross-functional selection teams. And they began the transition from "employees just working here" to "employees as owners and operators of their business."

It was clear that Paul and his team couldn't move the refinery from "underperforming" to "world class" in a single stage—the performance gap was too overwhelming. So a series of shaping steps was designed to ensure success. For example, the ultimate safety goal was zero reportable incidents, but the first target was set at a 50% improvement in employee and contractor incidents. Similar achievable goals were set for the other three areas.

After eight months, 90% of the refinery's managers and supervisors had successfully impacted their targeted behaviors. 85% successfully impacted their results target. Front-line supervisors and middle managers were successfully executing projects to positively influence behavior in the desired direction. (Examples: 100% of the refinery workers now wore their protective gear 100% of the time; environmental incidents were being spotted and curtailed faster than the industry standard required.)

In the months leading up to the PBL coaching, the refinery experienced total reportable incident rates (TRIR) as high as 2.0 per year, well above the target level of less than 1.0 per year. As a result of coaching action plans focused on critical path behaviors that drove the four results areas, the refinery experienced remarkable improvements:

- The safety incident rate dropped to 0.4 (0.26 for employees).

- Environmental exceedences decreased by 70%.

- Morale rose significantly; union grievances dropped from ten to zero.

- Utilization increased significantly.

- Off-spec product and incident cost (lost profit opportunity) decreased by 75%.

Following these achievements and sustained performance against the targets, they celebrated progress, and new targets supported by new critical path behaviors were selected by PBL participants. They focused on the next exciting and possible performance level, sustaining momentum, and keeping positive energy and morale on an upward spiral.

"We're seeing a real change in people, particularly the operators," Paul noted. "Management mistrust is decreasing, race relations are improving. We have clearly demonstrated that putting a positive focus on changing behavior does improve performance, but you need to set realistic goals in order to ultimately succeed."

Making Change Happen Consistently: The MAKE-IT™ MODEL

"Our transition from a functional organization to integrated business units was the right strategy, well-planned. We did well identifying new roles and responsibilities, changing core processes, and altering our structure. Many of us had been through this in other units. But the execution nearly killed us as we tried to make the new strategy work.

"We weren't prepared for the time needed to clarify 'what' and 'why.' We had to redeliver our communications daily. Lack of buy-in frustrated us and employees. Sales and customer satisfaction numbers faltered. Everyone blamed the re-org. Resistance to finishing the transition was immense; criticism of leadership was high.

"Our problems came down to this: we let old ways prevail, and nothing encouraged doing things 'the new way.' We greatly underestimated the need to manage behavioral changes to support the structural changes—and the need to have key metrics for tracking so we could quickly spot problems and focus efforts to resolve them. It's now clear that managing organizational change really means managing behavioral change across an entire organization."

—*Chief Operating Officer, Fortune 50 Company*

CHANGE HAS BECOME the operative word of our generation. We want to change everything for the better, to see things around us changed for good. We want to believe that change is always possible, and that we have the power to affect the world and how it operates.

We also expect to see change from our political leaders . . . from our organizational leaders . . . from those in key decision-making roles. In general, we live in a time when people expect to see constant change/improvement as a result of feedback and input.

But change is hard, especially when patterns of behavior are long-established. It's very challenging to get people to do things in a new way, and consistently. Even when people say they *want* to change, and *intend* to change, it doesn't mean they *can* or *will*. Many "change implementations" are well-purposed and intentioned, yet meet with disappointment, disenfranchisement, and unsustainability.

Nothing changes until people's behaviors change. No matter what you are trying to achieve, if people don't *do* things differently, change can't happen or be sustained.

MAKE-IT™ MODEL FOR ORGANIZATIONAL CHANGE

In this chapter, we will step away from the **IMPACT MODEL**, which guides individual performance improvement, and look at our model for *organization-level* improvement. We call it the **MAKE-IT™ MODEL**.

Its name refers to the four "Make-It" steps that it comprises: **Make It Clear, Make It Real, Make It Happen,** and **Make It Last.**

We have found over the years that achieving organization-wide behavioral change requires attention to additional variables beyond the scope of the **IMPACT MODEL** (e.g., leadership team alignment, development of an implementation and communications strategy, etc.).

Thus, we created the **MAKE-IT MODEL** for organizational change that encompasses these and other steps— but which has, at its core, the **IMPACT MODEL** for individual change.

(NOTE: The Make-It model is introduced and overviewed in this chapter. For more information, please visit www.clg.com.)

OVERVIEW: THE FOUR "MAKE-IT" STAGES

Here is a quick overview of the four stages—and your role in each.

1. Make It Clear

In *Make It Clear,* the strategic direction for the change is clearly laid out and agreed upon by the organization's senior leaders. Leaders **Identify** their highest-priority business opportunity and specify how they will **Measure** its achievement.

That becomes input to other leaders who work at the next levels down in the organization. *Make It Clear* is complete when all members of the leadership team are aligned and agree that they have identified:

- The right business opportunity upon which to focus change
- The right means of measuring progress for that opportunity
- The right key performers to drive the change in the organization
- And when they have committed to the right leadership behaviors.

This is where a *business case for change,* including the targeted results, is developed to inspire and motivate the organization to follow.

2. Make It Real

New results require new behaviors. So, the work in *Make It Real* is complete when all leaders confirm the results they are targeting for improvement—and when they identify the **Pinpoints** or the right behaviors to make it happen. This is also where preparation happens for "the right way" to get the right behaviors.

Leaders work hard to make real the change they are contemplating. They understand the organization's culture and what will enable or hinder the changes they are preparing to implement. The "P" for *pinpointing* here also could easily stand for *preparation*.

It is key here to "go slow to go fast" and not shortchange what it takes to mobilize effective behavioral change. Drill down to the behaviors necessary to achieve the targeted results, and the behaviors that must change. Ensure that leaders at all levels have the skills to give performance feedback to key performers quickly, reliably, and appropriately during *Make It Happen.*

Of course, you also must prepare leaders by giving them the skills to activate the right behaviors and ensure they are encouraged by positive consequences. Likewise, leaders must be comfortable in giving constructive coaching for undesired behaviors that are constraining the organization. As you have learned, you must not leave these encouraging/discouraging skills to chance—they don't occur naturally.

In *Make It Real*, we take steps (strategic communications, focus groups, training) to prepare leaders for key behaviors in the *Make It Happen* phase. These are all important to ensuring that key performers can exhibit the new behaviors you expect. Again, leaders' behavior in implementation is key. Ensure they have the support they need to navigate it well.

3. Make It Happen

The name of this stage says it all—*implementation! Make It Happen* requires lots of coaching and feedback on effective leadership behaviors, plus tracking of deployment success, and active removal of barriers incurred en route to bringing about the new change. Given such committed leadership, key performers will consistently accomplish their critical path behaviors and be prideful doing it.

This is not a delegation stage. It is a time when key leaders systematically **Activate** the right behaviors to get them started, and **Consequate** them to ensure they happen again. Leaders give positive feedback to performers who "implement the change," to encourage them along the way and address issues that inevitably arise.

Make It Happen is complete when the planning in *Make It Clear* and *Make It Real* bears fruit: behaviors of key performers and leaders improve, discretionary performance at all levels increases, and targeted results improve.

4. Make It Last

Make It Last

Transfer

Fluency to Sustain Behavior

This is the stage that—unfortunately—is often left out of most change implementations. *Make It Last* focuses on *sustaining* the change: transferring the new behaviors and new ways of working so they become the everyday standard of doing business. Some call it *"Make It Stick."* We think this step is so important that we have devoted a whole chapter to it (Chapter 8).

Make It Last requires embedding the approach and tools into your business planning, leadership development, strategic talent management, and whatever core processes drive your organization's work. You must be certain your HR functions are selecting for and systematically evaluating/encouraging the new behaviors.

A *lot* of leadership encouragement goes into *Make It Happen,* and this may need to continue, but with lighter touches and at longer intervals. Making change last requires organizational systems realignment to ensure that processes and systems are consistent with the new vision/ways of working—and are actively prompting and encouraging "the new way."

IT'S ABOUT OUTCOMES

Organizations that fully apply the **MAKE-IT MODEL** do so to achieve improvements in:

- **Business results**—rapid and measurable achievement of targeted results by fostering the critical few behaviors that truly make a difference.

- **Leadership effectiveness**—improved leadership and coaching skills for leaders at all levels, while they make things happen.

- **Execution**—faster, more consistent, more complete execution of strategic initiatives—or "stickiness in the field"—when rolling out new and improved processes.

- **Culture**—an environment that encourages desired behaviors and ensures there are sources of encouragement for employees getting "the right results, the right way."

Each of these improvements relies on aligning behaviors toward the same outcomes, so that success will be sustained because the behavioral approach becomes embedded in the culture.

Remember that change implementation is not about doing a bunch of "stuff" so you can say that you "did change management." It's not about checking-off activities. *Implementation is always about achieving real outcomes.*

Following each *Make-It* stage is a "gate," at which leaders rigorously assess progress. At these gates, leaders decide whether both they and their organization are ready to advance to the next stage. This is shown in the following figure.

THE STAGE-GATED IMPACT MODEL: FOUR STAGES TO SUCCESS

MAKE-IT™ Model
Outcomes for Implementation

Stage 1 Goal: Prioritize business opportunities

- Key leaders (and other sponsors supporting the change) understand Behavioral Science and their important role in coaching/supporting new behaviors.
- Senior leaders aligned to business opportunities and targeted results.

- Other key leaders (as needed) aligned to business opportunities/change being implemented.
- Business opportunities prioritized by high-ROI potential and fragility in implementation (requires focused effort for success).

Stage 1 Gate:
Senior leaders aligned on biz opps, targeted results, metrics?

Stage 2 Goal: Align organization to pinpointed behaviors & prepare leaders to execute

- All organizational levels aligned on key performers, pinpointed behaviors, targeted results.
- Next-level leaders and implementation field leaders prepared to support change.

- Results tracking systems operational to monitor success & quickly respond to issues.
- Leaders at all levels prepared to coach/give feedback on new behaviors.
- Leadership teams approve detailed change implementation plan.

Stage 2 Gate:
Ready to implement change?

Stage 3 Goal: Prompt and Encourage new behaviors to achieve new results

- Leadership teams (all levels) routinely using data to encourage change implementation & act on quick-fix areas.

- Evidence of desired leadership practices occurring, plus frequent feedback delivery (all levels).
- Sustainability Plan developed.

Stage 3 Gate:
Target results improving and positive cultural changes evident?

Stage 4 Goal: Integrate new behaviors into routine business processes

- New ways of working integrated into organization's management systems.

- Consequence systems aligned to consistently prompt & reinforce desired behaviors.

Stage 4 Gate:
New ways of working now business as usual?

There is a lot of flexibility in each stage, lots of ways to achieve the outcomes that enable passing through the stage gate. Just keep in mind that the outcomes are specific results that you and your leadership team must achieve before it is wise to enter the next stage.

The outcomes shown in the figure can seem sequential, but this is not the case. Rather, an effective leader of change implementation will:

- Work simultaneously on several outcomes in the current stage.

- Look ahead to outcomes in the next stage to lay their foundations.

- Look back to outcomes achieved in earlier stages, to continue making progress beyond what was required to pass through the gate.

A final note: large-scale change efforts generally take months or years to complete, and many steps are involved that we do not cover here. Also, much can happen during a change effort—business objectives may change, a new leader may appear, the organization may restructure. When you face a change of this magnitude, don't simply march on! Take the time to recycle back to the appropriate stage in the **MAKE-IT MODEL**.

YOUR ORGANIZATIONAL CULTURE

Change-focused leaders and implementers know that the single greatest problem in bringing about change is *entrenched culture*. Early in change implementation, it is key to understand your organization's culture and how it will enable or hinder your change effort.

To bring about behavioral change in your organization, look hard at its culture. We define culture like this:

> **Culture**
>
> is a pattern of behavior . . .
>
> that gets encouraged or discouraged . . .
>
> by the company's systems and/or people . . .
>
> over time.

Cultures get established whether we want them to or not. Ways of working, talking, managing, solving problems, and resolving issues become ingrained in an organization because "it's always been that way"—or said behaviorally, "because there are strong encouragers for the old behaviors, and nothing to discourage them."

Here is just how different the cultures of two companies can be—at all levels:

Cultural Component	Company A	Company B
Real work hours (not the official ones)	*People come early, stay late*	*People are expected to get the work done in whatever hours work best for them*
Signature authority	*The Chosen Few*	*We don't worry about getting signatures upfront. You are accountable only if something goes wrong.*
Dress	*Suits, ties, conservative*	*Business casual unless you are meeting with a customer that day*
Social interaction	*Politeness when required*	*Colleagues are genuinely courteous*
Communication	*Letters, e-mail*	*Voicemail, e-mail*
Lunchtime activities	*Eat at desk while reading e-mail*	*Eat with colleagues or work out*
Political landscape	*Palace intrigue; loose lips sink ships*	*Say it like it is. We value honesty in relationships*
Leave policy	*Rigid*	*Flexible, as long as the work gets covered*
Empowerment	*As long as you do it my way, all is well*	*Just do it*
Attitude toward customers	*Cater to our premier customers*	*We value all of our customers and want their handling to be seamless*
Restrooms	*Pristine*	*Out of paper again*
The boss' door	*Open by appointment only . . . and it had better be important!*	*Open to all*

Both Company A and Company B could be very successful. But just imagine trying to change the culture in either company—and how differently each company would react to the same strategy. Then, imagine a *merger* of these two cultures!

So, to change an organization, you first must understand how it currently behaves, and determine why—identify its sources for encouraging and discouraging behaviors.

Culture Resists Change

The resistance to changing entrenched culture—and the power of the behavioral approach to change it—is evident in this story from one of our clients:

> Our CEO had a very tough challenge: either significantly reduce operating costs and expense-related practices, or face losses from anticipated price erosion in the market. So his Cost Team did a corporate-wide study on cost reduction and cost management.
>
> They analyzed spending and investment patterns and recommended cost-reduction strategies in every area. The Cost Team worked hard and delivered a plump report detailing observations, findings, and cost-reduction opportunities.
>
> Then they told the CEO the very thing he didn't want to hear: *"Our expense issue is really a cultural issue. Our culture doesn't support cost focus and cost reduction. Most of our managers grew up in the growth side of the business. Further, our whole industry has been prospering. So, within the current culture, it will be tough to make inroads on cost reduction . . . ."*
>
> The CEO went ballistic. *"Culture,"* he proclaimed, *"is a nebulous, fuzzy, and weak excuse for poor performance!"* He ordered them never to mention the "C-word" again. And he told them to find the *real* problem and come back with recommendations that made sense.
>
> Tails between their legs, the Cost Team redid their work. They *knew* the problem was cultural, but in their data-driven world, they needed scientific proof for the CEO.
>
> The cost team went back to the CEO, but this time with Behavioral Science behind them. They sidestepped the word "culture" at first. They pointed out that the needed *behaviors*—cost-monitoring, evaluation of cost above other factors in decision-making, etc.—were not behaviors historically encouraged within their company. In fact, the *wrong* behaviors—those that ignored cost—were being encouraged simply because times were good.

(By the way, the name for such a pervasive pattern of behaviors that gets encouraged or discouraged by a company's systems or people over time is called, pardon the word, "culture.")

The CEO began to grasp that this was indeed a culture problem, and one that could yield to behavior analysis. If he wanted to change behaviors, he had to—

- Seek a different behavior pattern than what already existed in the organization
- Understand that powerful sources of encouragement already existed for the current behaviors
- Understand that powerful discouragers for new behaviors could discourage change.

Thus began a significant effort to change this corporation's behavior patterns. The key was to change the encouragers and discouragers provided by the organization's systems and by leaders at all levels—starting with the Big Guy himself, who hired our colleague Ned Morse as his executive coach.

At this CEO's retirement some five years later, he touted the coaching and culture change work as the turning point for propelling the company forward, and for profoundly changing him as a leader, husband, and father.

To our knowledge, this company's effort remains today the single largest systematic and systemic application of behavioral technology inside a major corporation. They undertook a major effort to first understand their culture and then to change it— and it worked!

MAKE-IT™ Model Reduces Refinery Cost

This massive Gulf Coast oil refinery—one of the U.S. top ten—was becoming less competitive due to the cost of fuel gas, which comprised 50–60% of its operating expenses. To separate crude oil components, refineries burn fuel gas, and furnaces must be carefully tuned and operated for efficiency. Employee behaviors are key to efficient operation.

Refinery management asked us to help solve their burning problem, knowing of our repeated success in using Behavioral Science to turn around declining operations. We sent consultant Charles Carnes to apply our **MAKE-IT™ Model.**

The Business Opportunity. "Cost management was a critical part of business plans," noted Carnes, "and an operations review identified furnace efficiency (fuel consumption) as a major cost-saving opportunity realizable through targeted behavior changes."

Make It Clear

Identify & **M**easure

Target Results

Carnes worked closely with leaders to verify that energy consumption was an ideal results target: it linked directly to the cost-management business opportunity (fuel was 50–60% of each business units' operating expenses), and it was an achievable goal that managers and operators could influence directly.

Make It Real

Pinpoint

Critical Few Behaviors

CLG aligned key performers and their critical path behaviors to the desired outcome. They replaced the old metric—"fuel consumption across the entire business unit"—with a new one that reflected real furnace operator behaviors: "individual furnace efficiency."

Make It Happen

Activate & **C**onsequate

Desired Behavior

They "made it happen" by:

1. *Setting Expectations*. Shift Team Leaders (STLs) agreed on pinpointed furnace-tuning behaviors and rolled them out to operators, asking for their commitment to efficiency.

Make It Last

Transfer

Fluency to Sustain Behavior

2. *Measuring Behavior and Results*. STLs and operators developed an online monitoring tool to calculate fuel gas consumed by each furnace. They monitored consumption savings daily, weekly, and monthly and developed checklists to monitor operator behavior.

(continued)

3. *Coaching and Providing Feedback.* STLs observed operators regularly and gave them coaching and feedback. They monitored furnace results daily and discussed behavior and results data at Business Plan review meetings.

The implementation set up long-term continuous self-improvement, based on constant measuring of key performance metrics and behaviors required to attain them. One leader noted, "The process benefited furnace efficiency so well that we are extending the approach to other performance issues."

Results. Desired furnace-tuning behaviors increased from 70% to 100%, remaining steady as operators grew more committed. Results appeared within three months, and the refinery achieved almost $2.8 million energy savings in less than a year.

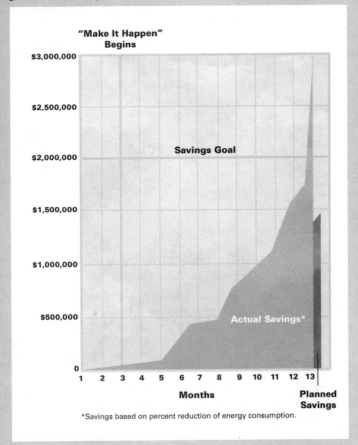

*Savings based on percent reduction of energy consumption.

BEHAVIORAL SUCCESS FACTORS BEHIND THE "MAKE-ITS"

Some organizations have a higher probability of success than others in implementing a new direction. We call such organizations "agile" or "more responsive to strategy change." Could they be lucky, or just that way by nature? Neither.

> ### Successful change implementation . . .
>
> is the result of a strategy execution effort that is guided by a clear purpose and metrics for success; is carefully planned for and communicated; is well-resourced and supported; and includes frequent feedback and encouragement for progress made.

In our overview of the four *Make-Its,* you saw that they constitute a science-based, proven model for successful change implementation. In fact, you can regard the *Make-Its* as "insurance policies" for success.

Let us now look more closely at each *Make-It* to discover specific keys that heavily influence successful implementation of that stage.

STAGE 1: MAKE IT CLEAR

Make It Clear

Identify &
Measure

Target Results

Understanding Your Corporate Culture & Consequence History

As part of *Make It Clear,* where you get leadership alignment on the strategy and key results to be achieved, you must work through some questions:

- What behaviors does our culture encourage?
- What happens *today* when unwanted behaviors occur?
- Does someone say or do anything?

- Do we look the other way if unwanted behavior comes from a person or group whose business unit is making money?

There are almost always practices that go on inside organizations that no one wants to talk about—but that are important to acknowledge and be willing to change, so that a successful change implementation can take hold. Failure to identify these elements—or worse, failure to talk about them openly among leaders—is a sure-fire way to show the organization you are not *really* going to change.

Everyone knows what the elephant in the room is! So, name it, address it, deal with it. To make the new strategy clear and gain alignment on it, it is key to provide an honest look at the organization today—and what drives it.

Understanding Consequence History

To really understand how a change initiative will be received by the organization, you must first understand people's behavioral history in your organization. It is important to understand the baseline from which they are starting—through their eyes.

In general, for most people, the antecedents associated with change initiatives have generated a pretty negative consequence history. Too many times, people are told: "Trust me." "This will be a good thing." "I will change all of that." "You will be minimally impacted." "Your support will be critical to this effort." "We want to understand what happened, but we don't want anyone to feel blamed."

All of that sounds good—but what many people hear is, "Here we go again." "Change for change's sake." "Same old stuff." "Nothing in it to make my world better."

Once you know the consequence history in your organization, you can develop *behavior-shaping plans* that will ensure *positive consequences* for the new behaviors that you ask of people. There are many steps between "here's what we are going to do" and "we are truly making it happen."

STAGE 2: MAKE IT REAL

Implementing Change: Forget Supply-Push—Create Demand-Pull

The work in *Make It Real* is complete when all leaders are prepared for the change and aligned on *the what* and *the how*. This is also where the method for deployment/implementation is determined.

We cannot emphasize enough how important the implementation strategy is, and how key it is to take the time needed to prepare it well. What will be most effective at engaging the hearts and minds of our people—even as we are changing?

Most organizations use a traditional cascading approach when implementing new strategies. Changes start at the top with high-level executives and cascade systematically downward into the organization—with the intent of ensuring that the leadership above understands and can model the new, desired behaviors. This makes perfect sense and creates a logical, orderly approach to change. However, it doesn't work.

In our company, we call this "supply-push," and we think it's a recipe for failure. With supply-push, a group has something it wants others to do—commonly referred to as a "new initiative." New things that need to be done are pushed top-down throughout the organization. This usually is done irrespective of whether people want it, need it, or use it. Resistance becomes intense (if passive), and people begin engaging in the desired new behaviors just enough to delay or avoid punishment for "not being on board."

You should immediately recognize supply-push implementation as likely to encourage behaviors that will only get *discouraged*. In other words, people will engage only in enough behavior related to the new initiative to avoid being an "opposer" or "non-supporter," but rarely will they engage in enough behavior to really make the thing work. In a couple of our client companies, they call this "dodging the silver bullet."

We have been referring to the line between discouragement and encouragement as the point where discretionary performance begins. And we want to create want-to work environments in this have-to world. So, if supply-push doesn't work, how do you implement a new initiative? How do you help people want to change?

To Make It Happen, Create Demand-Pull

If you want people to change, they must see what's in it for them. How will it benefit their business or their lives? For most managers and executives, the opportunity to decide what is good, or not, for your organization is a huge positive consequence. With demand-pull, you can build this into the process.

Like supply-push, demand-pull typically also begins with top leadership. Modeling desired behaviors or processes at the top is essential. However, you need to be concerned with the *encouragers* for engaging in the new behaviors. In addition, you need to *demonstrate the initiative's goodness* to earn the right to implement it across the whole organization.

You demonstrate its goodness by pursuing a dual path of implementation with top leadership *and* with the organization. While educating, coaching, framing, and learning occurs with the organization's top leaders, you also provide opportunities for key groups lower in the organization to lead the charge. These are groups predisposed to try the new approach, to participate early in the change process—groups whose success matters to the business and whose performance is visible to others.

If the new ways of doing things are worthwhile—if they lead to meaningful change and improvement, if they are truly worth the time and dollars people must invest in them—then results will follow. Behaviors will change at the local level and targeted results will improve.

And these changes, together with positive reports to senior management, will serve two main functions:

1. They will encourage sponsorship behaviors on the part of the senior team, which is just beginning its own learning process.

2. They will stimulate demand-pull from other parts of the organization, which will want to have (and eventually will embrace) what helped other divisions or departments improve.

Demand-pull implementation strategies put the burden on those implementing the change to be excellent, efficient, relevant, and results-oriented. The implementers reward the parts of the organization that need assistance and want to improve their performance. They also create an unparalleled group-level support for the change, which spreads quickly—for the right reasons. Finally, they keep behaviors and results closely linked to ensure that time invested is returned in the most profitable way.

STAGE 3: MAKE IT HAPPEN

Shape, Shape, Shape Behavior

The most common issue we see in the *Make It Happen* phase is *failure to recognize and encourage progress toward the desired state.* It is so key during the heat of change—when all kinds of issues and challenges arise—to recognize and celebrate desired behaviors that *are* happening, and to encourage progress toward the desired end.

We always say that "implementing change" is not for the faint-hearted. It requires a lot of in-the-trenches work—talking with people, helping them understand why, earning their trust through real listening and engagement, and helping to make sure that the implementation happens as it should.

Ensure you have effective antecedents in place. Walk the halls. Use email and voicemail. Communicate five times as much. Ensure you have consequences and feedback providers ready to encourage desired behaviors. It's key to actively appreciate those who are working their tails off to make the change happen.

Don't leave new behaviors to chance. Encourage them every chance you get. And show up to redirect the unwanted behaviors that inevitably will surface during the *Make It Happen* phase.

A Note About Executive Sponsorship

The desired behaviors of executive sponsors during a major change effort involve engagement, communications, support, and sponsorship. It is important that each organization understands what behaviors are most critical for their leaders to exhibit, given their organization's culture.

These desired behaviors of executive sponsors can be prompted and encouraged by coaching, for a while. But the behaviors eventually need to come under the control of the biggest natural consequences that the executive finds rewarding: observable behavioral/cultural changes—and improved bottom-line performance of the organization.

So, if improvement in culture and bottom-line results is not detected within months after implementation, "sponsorship" behaviors fail to get encouraged, diminish in frequency and intensity, and may stop.

Don't get surprised like this. Executives operate under tremendous pressure. If they don't see improvements quickly, they begin seeking other "silver bullets" . . . and thus continues the cycle of negative consequences for trying new change behaviors in the organization.

We really recommend designing-in leading indicators of progress so you know early if things are tracking correctly or not. You don't want to wait a moment longer than you need to—to know if there are issues that need to be addressed.

STAGE 4: MAKE IT LAST

Align Consequence Systems

A final insurance policy for consolidating your gains made during *Make It Clear,* *Make It Real,* and *Make It Happen* is to Transfer the sources of encouragement for the new behaviors to ensure they are sustained. This is done primarily by skilled leaders and with consequence systems operating within an organization.

Aligning consequence systems with what you are trying to achieve is a necessary step to sustaining progress in the *Make it Last* stage. Sustaining change, support, and sponsorship at all levels requires that consequence systems (pay, promotion, recognition, development) support the new behaviors and do not compete with what you are trying to do by encouraging the wrong behaviors. This makes sure that things go right.

To illustrate, here's what can go wrong:

> One of our clients asked for help in developing leadership skills and processes to improve bottom-line results. We worked hard for 18 months to educate, coach, and support hundreds of leaders, from the company president to the front-line shift supervisors. They learned new ways of managing the business. They were told that future success in the company depended heavily on leadership skills and how well they managed people.

> But as the leadership and human resources people worked on changing the job selection and promotion processes, teams continued to use policies from the old culture to select people for promotion and high-potential opportunities. The company risked contradicting the new way by continuing to reward and promote the old way.

> Fortunately, it wasn't long before they implemented, revised, and aligned systems for performance appraisal, compensation, recognition, and job promotion. They also adjusted the

**requirements for progression to ensure that all promotions,
visible and invisible, strengthened the new culture.**

If reward and recognition systems are not adjusted to reinforce the behaviors identified in key initiatives, the initiatives
will fail. Behaviors will not be reinforced and sustained in the
long run. And repeated failure perpetuates the cycle of change
that is "not made to last."

Realistically, at the outset, you may be limited to assuring
that the consequence systems are not working against you by
supporting undesired behaviors. You can later improve the
consequence systems so they encourage the new desired behaviors. This can increase the rate of new behaviors and sustain
them.

Think for a moment about your own organization. What
behaviors are *officially* valued, versus the ones that *actually* get
encouraged? The table offers some common examples to help
you.

What the organization <u>says</u> . . .	What the organization <u>does</u> . . .
"We value diversity"	The norm is to promote white males who have been with the organization a long, long time.
"Teamwork is valued and important"	Financial incentives and promotions are determined by individual accomplishments and outcomes.
"We care about people"	Bonuses are contingent upon bottom-line results, regardless of how they are achieved.
"Work-family balance is important"	Staying late, working weekends, taking laptop on vacation, and checking voicemail seven days per week is expected. Employees who don't do this are described as lazy.
"We offer free checking!"	No fee is charged for checking at local bank; remote check-cashing or ATM usage incurs a service charge.
"Safety is our first priority"	Near-misses that allow the line to continue running and don't lead to shutting down are seen as heroic.

I'll bet you could create a page-full of similar examples from your own company!

The bottom line: implementation requires behavior change. Behavior change is a function of what people and systems (pay, promotion, selection, rewards) either encourage (through positive consequences) or discourage (through negative consequences), whether intentional or unintentional. In order to *Make It Last*, you need to ensure that consequence systems reinforce desired behaviors.

What we encourage, we get. What we discourage, we don't get. It's just that simple.

UNLOCK BEHAVIOR, UNLEASH (NOT-FOR-) PROFITS

We have focused on profit-making enterprises, but not-for-profits can "profit" every bit as much from applying Behavioral Science to improve performance. Our colleague Carolina Aguilera recounts her experience in applying the **MAKE-IT MODEL** in a faith-affiliated nursing/hospice facility . . .

> This facility provided quality care, created a caring environment, and collaborated with the community. But they had internal ailments: absenteeism, turnover, medication errors, culture conflicts, red ink. The problems distressed everyone, particularly in this spiritual setting. So, I applied our MAKE-IT™ MODEL . . .
>
> - *Make It Clear.* I surveyed the staff, unearthing problems of accountability, communication, priorities, departmental silos, and inadequate resources. This research helped them clearly understand issues, prioritize strategic objectives, and target results for improvement.
> - *Make It Real.* They saw that success lay in positively encouraging key performers for doing the right critical path behaviors—crucial actions likely to occur only if focused leadership was applied.
> - *Make It Happen.* I taught them Behavioral Science principles, customized for their situation. I developed every

manager as a Performance Coach, and the top adminis-
trator and a nursing director as internal coaches.

- *Make It Last.* They achieved this by integrating performance
  management skills into the organization's future. The
  MAKE-IT MODEL is now an integral part of their business
  management, and they are training all new managers in
  behavioral methodology.

Results

The client told us, "Your outreach during this critical period in
our history was so beneficial. It helped our organization grow.
The biggest benefit was development of our managers, who
learned behavior analysis, giving them a new problem-solving
structure. They also learned ways of coaching and the value of
encouragement. They acquired key tools for improving
employees' behavior.

"Our turnover dropped dramatically, and we have good
results in quality and family satisfaction. We keep using the
tools, and helping new managers grow through their use. Our
Board is very supportive, and expects us to continue using the
behavioral tools.

"The proof is in the numbers: 70% medication error reduction,
sharply reduced cost, 25% reduced call-offs, etc.

"Our consultant, Carolina, helped us find ways to more
effectively communicate our mission. She was a real Godsend,
with great insights and great coaching through some difficult
times."

The **MAKE-IT MODEL** works equally well in corporations,
small businesses, hospitals, universities, schools—any organization that runs on people.

TAKEAWAYS ON THE MAKE-IT MODEL

1. The four MAKE-ITS guide you through the change-implementation steps to change behaviors across and within your organization—

Make It Clear: Identify and prioritize business opportunities and ways to measure target results. Understand your organization's culture and consequence history to ensure your change is set up to succeed.

Make It Real: Align the organization on the desired results—and the critical few behaviors needed for success. Think through the implementation method that is best for what you are trying to achieve—and that takes into account the organization's history.

Make It Happen: Activate, consequate, and shape, shape, shape behavior. Be visible. Be an engaged leader who is helping the organization to change—one behavior, one person, one team, one work unit, one division, one company at a time.

Make It Last: Sustainability is key—and you must be sure that the organizational systems and processes are encouraging the (new) behaviors desired by the company.

2. Several steps embedded in the Make-Its ensure successful change management—

- **Understand your organization's culture and consequence history (part of Make It Clear).** Entrenched culture is the great challenge to change. Leaders and employees are numb to antecedents, with a consequence history so powerful, and often negative, that traditional management cannot overcome it. Understanding this helps you deliver fresh antecedents and consequences to implement the new change with success.

- **Use demand-pull strategy rather than supply-push for implementing change (part of Make It Real).** Persuade people to implement the change by focusing on what's in it for them (demand) and delivering on your promises. Demand-pull usually requires a dual path of implementation with top leadership and the organization. While working with leaders, also provide opportunities for key groups lower in the organization to participate. Behaviors will change at the local level, and targeted results will improve.

- **Shape, shape, shape behavior! Don't leave consequences to chance (part of Make It Happen).** Catch people doing the right things, the right way—and let them know it. Be visible, remove barriers, help the organization navigate through the change process.

- **Align consequence systems with what you are trying to achieve (part of Make It Last).** Ensure that consequence systems (pay, promotion, recognition, development) are encouraging the right behaviors, not the wrong ones, which would compete with your goal.

Highlighting Excellence . . .

A Great Turnaround at Heinz

An interview with Dave Moran, President of Heinz Consumer Products. Dave & his team transformed the business, culture, and leadership structure of this $3B division of the H.J. Heinz Company, creating an amazing organization that is a leader among peers.

"**D**espite the company's powerhouse brands, we were declining in sales, volume, profit—virtually every metric. The organization was not well aligned. We were not pursuing good ideas, and the ideas we were going after were outside of the core business.

When I took over as President, the core business was ailing. Brands were in decline and our competition had leapfrogged us.

Worse, we lacked a high-quality team leading this division. For several decades, we had not invested in people, work processes, and how we worked. Ours was not an organization where, frankly, people wanted to be. We had lost a trusting environment that had made this company so strong—and we needed to get it back.

Our Chairman challenged me and the leadership team to (1) get these wonderful staples of American households moving again and create profitable growth, (2) get the malaise out, and (3) dramatically improve the predictability of the business.

The key was Number 2—getting the malaise out—because it drove the other two: profitable growth and predictability. So we started with the people.

We spent a lot of time *Making It Clear* and laying out what our Big Six Objectives were. We engaged CLG at the beginning when we were mapping out direction. I am grateful for that, because they helped us settle on a course that would lead to the company's turnaround, and that path we are still following today, five years later.

As we moved to *Make It Real,* we did a lot of work identifying which were the proper behaviors to drive the business, how people worked and how they connected across the organization. On day one, Leslie said to me, "You really have two choices on how to win." So I dutifully wrote "1," and she said, "You can change the people." Then I wrote "2," and she said, "Or you can change the people." Given those two options, I decided to change the people!

Of all my direct reports, all but one was replaced. Three were found within the organization, and with the promise that we were going to change the culture, we recruited four from first-class consumer goods companies. They understood how to move an organization, how to win in the marketplace, and how to help make this new culture a reality.

But we also had 865 salaried employees at headquarters. Morally, I didn't want to change out those people—and, frankly, they weren't the problem. So, in terms of the other 'changing of the people,' I learned a very valuable lesson about bringing everyone along as we *made it happen*. And while we did have to make key changes, I was pleased that 500 of those employees decided to stay, to get with the program, move in tandem with the organization, and work the way we wanted the new culture to operate.

It was not enough to say, "we want you to change." It was not enough for us to just encourage people to do things differently. We had to show, to coach, and to teach. In other words, we had to lead—and that began with me.

The leadership team chose to *Make It Happen* by owning the reorganization and leading from the top, rather than telling people to just make the numbers. We (the leadership team) had set the numbers, so we had to work with the organization to be sure we delivered them. We worked with the organization to bring new ideas to win in the marketplace.

When you are hiring this many new people and transforming an organization, it is all about changing the work, the behaviors, and belief system. Being a 140-year-old company is both a benefit and a hindrance. The culture was very entrenched, and highly siloed. Sales didn't work well with marketing, marketing didn't work well with R&D, and so on.

We instituted a lot of changes to address this, to become a high-performing work unit that believed in each other first and then could win in the marketplace. My role was to encourage truth, and I spoke bluntly: we are going to focus on the things that matter most; we are going to recognize real problems and solve them together; and we will celebrate progress every step of the way.

I can assure you that our company was floundering not because people didn't try—we were trying very hard. But the organization had not been focused on the right things.

In the past, people were reprimanded for missing numbers, so they were reluctant to bring forward problems when we still had time to fix them.

We had to change that about our culture—in other words, that pattern of behavior. We had to encourage people who brought forward the real issues early in the process. We had to model working issues together.

One of the great directives Leslie gave me was to "objectify the problem and use data." Today, even still, I go to no meetings with people to whom I report without objectifying the problem and using numbers—not pages of numbers, maybe just one page, but the truth is always in numbers—and we can objectify any situation quickly in a non-blaming way. My team also now applies this model in working with me. All of this was part of *Making It Happen.*

A phrase that always stops a meeting and makes us pause and reflect is "what problem are we trying to solve?" That's a phrase I use almost every day. We are very clear now, always, about what problem we are trying to solve—and what behaviors we are trying to influence.

In our business, taste is number one for a reason. We have been very busy upgrading the quality of our products so the consumer experience is better and better. We focused on innovation and improving our customer service. We focused on top-line growth—and we worked very hard at cutting non-value-added costs. We are working always on developing the leadership pipeline and talent in our organization. It all starts and ends with the quality of people who have signed on to the change.

My key learnings through all of this were:

1. *We all wait too long to address people problems.* We agonize over them, awake at 3:00 A.M. thinking about them. But we will not win unless we get the right people in the right jobs and create the right environment for them to be successful.

2. *Feedback is the cheapest, fastest, and most effective way to change behavior.* After a meeting, a quick email, a quick voicemail, a quick handwritten note provides immediate feedback. We have so many tools today to deliver feedback; quickly, easily and effectively—we just need to use them. Feedback is the key to it all.

   My first few years on this job, there was a lot of negative feedback: "stop doing this, do something different." Now that we have turned the company around, a lot of my feedback is "please continue, you are going exactly down the right path," or "I am particularly excited about X and Y—how did you make it happen?"

3. *Trust your team, or get a new one.* Trust up and down is vital. I won't ever work in an organization again where trust is not rampant. I require it from my team. I need it from my boss, I give it myself. And I am pretty uncompromising about it.

4. *Find trusted advisors.* Believe in them and listen to them. It doesn't mean you're asking them to make your decisions; it doesn't mean you are abdicating your responsibility. I know some people who say, "gosh, it's lonely at the top." Well, there have been days when I have felt alone, and those were the days that I failed to turn to friends and advisors who really care about us and our organization and who can truly help."

This effort has paid off handsomely: Dave's division has averaged double-digit profit growth since Fiscal 2003. Fiscal 2006 was the strongest year yet, with sales up 13%.

Creating the IMPACT Culture— Make It Last

"Over five years, we encouraged new behaviors to transform our organization—from siloed and dead-average competitively, to a customer-focused, high-performing, leader-led, teamwork-supported entity that crossed organizational and functional boundaries. We kicked butt on every key metric, led the pack vs. competitors, and were positioned to continue growing market share and adding manufacturing capacity.

"Then our CEO became ill and had to step down, with no short-term planning for CEO succession. The Board brought in a seasoned CEO from outside—but his interest/passion for how *we did things was nearly nonexistent. He was 'old school.' He came in to do a big deal, to make us bigger and more profitable at any cost.*

"It was the truest test of our culture-and-practices sustainability that we could have had. We now had a leader at the top who cared only that we made our numbers—and who had no patience for understanding that how we made our numbers was all about encouraging behaviors that mattered— up, down, and across the company."

—EVP, Operations, Fortune 100 Company

THE CHALLENGE with any change effort, personal or organizational, is how to sustain it—*Make It Last*. This means embedding the new behaviors into everyday practice, so the improved results are sustained and built upon, and so new practices are passed on to future generations.

Let us revisit the **IMPACT MODEL** for its final step: **Transfer** fluency to sustain behavior. Sustaining both individual and organizational change is a real challenge—and fragile. Individuals must become fluent in managing behaviors, and organizations must ensure that the systems and processes maintain the right environment and encouragers for the "new way." In the **MAKE-IT MODEL,** this is part of *Make It Last.*

Just as Jack Welch created a "Six Sigma culture" at GE, you want to create an **IMPACT culture** in your company. You want the **IMPACT MODEL** to inform everything you and your employees do, every day. And you want that change to last beyond your tenure.

Here you face a different issue from those addressed in previous chapters. Until now, we've talked about effecting powerful change and getting powerful results from it. But now we shift focus to embedding **IMPACT** so deeply into your organization that it drives all business, with benefits to leaders, employees, customers, and ultimately shareholders.

CHANGING YOURSELF, CHANGING CULTURE: TWO SIDES OF THE SAME COIN

Creating a cultural shift is like changing your personal lifestyle.

For example, consider changing from a non-exerciser to working out three times a week. At first, you need to create special **Antecedents**: finding a place to work out, maybe people to share it with, and crafting a program to meet your timetable and goals.

More important, you need new **Consequences**. You need lots of **Encouraging, Immediate** consequences of **High Importance** that are **Likely** to occur (remember E-TIP). These consequences include encouragement from spouse, friends, and maybe your physician or co-workers. Maybe you track the minutes per week you work out.

Once in the groove of working out, you enjoy the personal benefits that sustain your behavior. You no longer need the same types of **Antecedents** and **Consequences**. You feel better, have higher energy, and are proud of how you look. You have a new set of conversations with people—and perhaps even new buddies to work out with. No need for special antecedents to get you to the gym.

And the consequences? They don't come so much from external sources any more . . . they come from inside of you and are powerful—how you feel and what you now can do. Positive consequences may still come from others who are encouraging the "new you," or from the mirror! But these external consequences are far less powerful than those that come from within.

Exercise has advanced from not part of your day, or even dreaded, to something you look forward to and enjoy. Exercising has its own inherent **Encouraging, Immediate** consequences of **High Importance** and **Likelihood** to you. And that is what will sustain your new behaviors.

Now, here is the parallel: in creating a culture change, you are after that same shift, from *planful* antecedents and consequences, to *natural* antecedents and consequences. The natural ones will sustain the change beyond the tenure of any one leader.

(By the way, this is why companies that try to "acquire" a high-performing culture by hiring away one or two executives don't get what they pay for. They get talented executives, but they can't get the culture those talented folks came from.)

COMPARING TWO CULTURES

Cultures in transition look different from a sustained **IMPACT** culture. Here are some of the differences in antecedents, behaviors, and consequences.

ANTECEDENTS	
Culture in Transition	**Sustainable IMPACT Culture**
• Leaders often provide simple, clear messages on goals & behaviors	• Messages on critical path behaviors embedded in routine statements of vision, mission, and in routine business planning/implementation
• Infrastructures in transition to support change (training, tracking systems)	
• New agreements formed (within teams; cross-functions; with customers)	• Business implementation plans include alignment of results targets & specify key performers and critical path behaviors
• Processes in transition to support new behavior & <u>not</u> old behavior	• Infrastructures, team & customer agreements, work processes support critical path behaviors

BEHAVIORS	
Culture in Transition	**Sustainable IMPACT Culture**
• Behaviors are new for leaders, supervisors, and key performers: people might feel less confident; work can take longer	• Leaders, supervisors, key performers fluent in critical path behaviors
	• Employees skilled in giving positive & constructive feedback
	• Employees show discretionary effort

CONSEQUENCES

Culture in Transition	Sustainable IMPACT Culture
• Leaders and peers provide many **Encouraging, Immediate, Highly Important, Likely** consequences for <u>new</u> behaviors	• Natural work consequences, peer feedback, & self-feedback sustain routine work performance
• Supervisors provide **Discouraging, Immediate, Highly Important, Likely** consequences for <u>old</u> behaviors	• Leaders, peers, & supervisors give occasional feedback on routine performance
• Leaders use natural consequences (built into the change itself)	• Leaders & peers give **Encouraging, Immediate, Highly Important, Likely** feedback for discretionary effort (on-the-spot recognition, awards)
• Leaders use self-consequences (give people access to info & feedback they need to self-evaluate)	• Organizational systems—HR, Finance, IT—support desired behavior by providing organization-level consequences
• Feedback from sponsors on improved behavior and how it leads to goals	

YOUR LEGACY: WILL IT BE A MUCH BETTER ORGANIZATION (COMPARED TO WHAT YOU INHERITED)?

If you're out for a quick win for yourself, ignore the advice in this book. And when you leave, the new approaches you've put in place will also leave, and any changes you made will surely evaporate.

In the end, leaders are evaluated by whether certain outcomes were realized while they were at the helm. Thus, leaders will do almost anything to realize those outcomes. Leaders also have control over many consequence systems—and it is those consequence systems that will ensure that things are "locked in" or maintained long after they depart.

The "new ways of working," if aligned with consequence systems, get baked into how work gets done, instead of needing a mandate or initiative from the new leader. And the more independent of you the new ways of working are, the greater the chance those new behaviors will continue after you move on to your next promotion!

MAKE IT LAST: BUILDING THE IMPACT CULTURE

Make It Last happens when the organization sustains the improvements it made through **IMPACT MODEL** implementation. Embedding the new ways/tools/approaches into the organization's business planning and leadership development processes is the key to sustaining them. New leaders must adopt the winning methods as the standard way of doing business.

In an **IMPACT culture**, the model is used on multiple levels. The figure shows how, depicting an annual business cycle. The cycle begins with clear direction from the highest level—from a corporate body, in this case. Planning proceeds in a systematic way to establish clear corporate goals with the critical few metrics released to business units.

Making It Last—sustainability—comes from repeated use of IMPACT™ at multiple levels in the organization

In the next step, leaders prioritize their business opportunities aligned with the corporate goals, and cascade results targets through the organization. (You'll recognize this as the first step of **IMPACT: Identify & Measure,** and you are familiar with the rest of the model from implementation.)

The key point on sustainability is to think of this cycle as equally applicable to the ongoing work of teams and even individuals. Every leadership team meeting should include, in reduced form, the elements of *Make It Clear, Make It Real,* and *Make It Happen.*

Suppose you are in the middle of your fiscal year and are attending a leadership team meeting. What should it look like in an **IMPACT culture?** There should be well-established business opportunities and quantified results targets that every team member knows. There should be current data on how well the team is meeting those targets. Every team member should understand and be able to openly, honestly discuss how well the team is doing. And by meeting's end, none should doubt what their best and highest focus should be for the next period.

In an **IMPACT culture,** the team doesn't just note progress and move on, or point fingers at people when results aren't great. The discussion is full of Behavioral Science as members speak objectively about what is going right—or wrong—and deliberately suggest changes in antecedents and consequences.

Leaders in an **IMPACT culture** hold similar, but less-formal conversations with their direct reports whenever they can. Instead of, "Hey, how's it going?" leaders approach people with questions like, "Hey, I saw that great production leap— congratulations! Tell me how you got that—and what your team did to make sure everyone still worked safely!" One-on-ones with direct reports offer the opportunity to give pinpointed acknowledgment and ongoing shaping.

In both instances—a team meeting and a leader talking with a direct report—leaders used the **IMPACT MODEL.**

WHERE DOES "TRANSFER AND SUSTAINABILITY" FIT?

Transferring new skills, or *Make It Last,* is also where "look-backs" are conducted to extract key learnings and build them into future implementations. Even the act of pulling together key people to discuss "How did the implementation go?" and "What could we have done better?" signals a valuing of the implementation effectiveness—as well as conveying an expectation that such learnings will be built into future executions.

Implementing change requires continuous learning. With every change effort, improvements will be made, new learnings brought in, refinements understood. Pause to ensure that the organization learns from this effort. Be sure that managing behavior through implementing (new) strategies becomes second nature to people. It is key to realizing change well.

Leaders focused on sustainability of performance improvements always seek fragile performance areas that could be solidified with a behavior-based approach. They ask:

- "Where are we vulnerable, performance-wise—and how do we ensure consequence-alignment with desired behaviors?"

- "What sources of encouragement exist for the new way of operating? What will ensure that these new behaviors get sustained?"

They are focused on aligning consequence systems and leadership practices to the new way of operating.

The key is to implement system changes that maintain and encourage employees' continued discretionary performance in areas important to the company.

Some of the best leaders we have worked with use the **Transfer** stage *(Make It Last)* as a prompt to return to the beginning, where they examine key performance outcomes they are trying to achieve, performances important to the organization, and start over with **Align & Measure** (the *Make It Clear* stage). The tool we use most often for this is the DCOM™ Model.

DCOM™ MODEL: KEY IMPLEMENTATION TOOL

The DCOM™ Model is a highly beneficial tool used by many of our consultants and clients to ensure that they consider the antecedents and consequences that are levers of high performance. Whether you are planning to execute a new strategy, or evaluating how the organization is currently performing, DCOM helps.

Distilled from Research on High-Performing Organizations

In response to the need for a simple, accurate tool for assessing the performance of organizations, DCOM was developed through research conducted independently by several organizations, aided by our colleague, Dr. James Hillgren. He named the model DCOM (pronounced "D-Com") for its four elements: Direction, Competence, Opportunity, and Motivation.

Each organization wanted to determine what was needed to get to the "next level." In one company, the "next level" meant moving total shareholder return from the bottom quartile to the top quartile in the industry. In another company, the "next level" meant making the organization a preferred national defense contractor.

Each company worked independently, studying organizations in various industries that had sustained high performance over several years. They compared practices of these companies against those of companies whose performance was mediocre or not sustained at high levels.

In each case, four key elements emerged that consistently distinguished sustained high performers, regardless of industry: **Direction, Competence, Opportunity,** and **Motivation— DCOM.**

The companies then applied the concepts to themselves and experienced dramatic changes in their own performance. As hoped, one company moved from the bottom quartile into the top quartile in shareholder return. Another company was recognized with the Malcolm Baldrige Award for quality.

The Four Elements of the DCOM™ Model

1. Direction—this is the "operationalization" of vision, mission, and values that results in a clear focus, priorities, and the alignment of all employee group efforts. It has four parts:

- An organizational sense of purpose that is meaningful to employees at all levels, resulting in every employee understanding how his/her job adds value.
- Values that go beyond the "screen saver"—values that have been behavioralized and are used to evaluate management decisions and actions.
- A performance measurement system focused on how value is delivered to the customer.
- A limited set of priorities, often just one to three.

2. Competence—the employees' and the organization's capabilities for managing and conducting work and work processes. Competence refers to the necessary skills to collaborate with one another, plus economic literacy at all levels—understanding the operating and financial leverage points of the company.

3. Opportunity—availability of resources, such as technology, process design, time, finance, and empowerment. Opportunity means having the right level of authority to act, clear boundaries, and the ability to refine and adapt work processes to enable performers to operate more efficiently. Opportunity includes access to resources needed to perform well.

4. Motivation—leaders' use of consequences to create an environment where people "want to," rather than "have to," perform at high levels. Motivation is the lynchpin in DCOM. It is the driver or energy in the system. It has three essential components:

- Real-time data-based feedback to all performers.

- Effective design and management of positive and negative consequences. (The research showed high-performing companies have solid alignment between the direction they give and the consequences people experience for their work. In mediocre companies, employees experience consequences not aligned with the direction.)

- In addition to solidly aligning consequences with direction, high-performing companies also need to align consequences with one another. Consequences that people experience from their superiors are consistent with those delivered through formal systems like compensation.

You can see that the first three elements (Direction, Competence, Opportunity) are a way to organize the antecedents for behavior. The last element, Motivation, focuses on the all-important consequence systems.

Hitting on All Four

The following chart shows the impact of each DCOM element on performance, and what happens when any one is missing.

D	C	O	M	**Results**
✓	✓	✓	✓	High Performance
✗	✓	✓	✓	Chaos
✓	✗	✓	✓	Bankruptcy
✓	✓	✗	✓	Frustration
✓	✓	✓	✗	Lethargy

Organization 1—Chaos. This organization has tremendous skills (Competence), resources (Opportunity), and enthusiastic employees (Motivation). But it lacks Direction, so chaos ensues. Without clear direction, employees work on the wrong things and business results deteriorate—along with employee morale.

Talented people soon leave for companies that have a clearer sense of purpose.

Organization 2—Bankruptcy. This organization's CEO builds a brilliant business strategy and communicates an inspiring, clear vision. His leadership team aligns results targets and critical path behaviors and thereby establishes strong Direction. Together, the leadership team provides additional resources for the change effort (Opportunity) and puts powerful consequences in place for achieving results (Motivation). But the leaders fail to recognize that their employees lack the necessary skills (Competence) to demonstrate the critical path behaviors. This scenario is a formula for bankruptcy: a major investment that relies on asking people to do something they can't!

Organization 3—Frustration. In this organization, people have clear Direction and are Competent and Motivated. But the Opportunity to do the work—time, equipment, or processes—doesn't allow them to get the work done. One supervisor spends time at home responding to emails, because he had 24 direct reports. That's a problem of Opportunity!

Organization 4—Lethargy. This culture lacks **Encouragers** to Motivate, or overuses **Discouragers,** leading to a workforce that puts forth minimal effort or is led primarily through coercion. At best, you get mediocre results.

The top row illustrates what happens when you are hitting on all four: high performance, and a sustainable organization.

"GETTING IT" IS THE EASY PART . . .

But "keeping it" is the true test of high-performing organizations.

Behaviors that are followed by positive consequences increase in frequency. That's what the science teaches us—so adding positive consequences and seeing an increase in behavior is not a big deal. Anyone should be able to make that happen, right?

So if we want to *sustain* a new behavior, we only need to make sure there are positive consequences for that behavior—or that the performer's behavior comes under control of natural self-provided consequences that are positive/encouraging. Right?

The problem is that attention to that level of behavior management is rarely done. It's easy to become focused on the initiative du jour—or with a leader change, to be chasing what the leader is driving . . . so that, even with the best intentions, the old way creeps back in.

MAKE-IT™ Model

Make It Clear

Identify & **M**easure
Target Results

Make It Real

Pinpoint
Critical Few Behaviors

Make It Happen

Activate & **C**onsequate
Desired Behavior

Make It Last

Transfer
Fluency to Sustain Behavior

Some of our most successful clients have developed peer feedback systems to ensure many sources of encouragement for new/desired behaviors, and not rely just on supervisor feedback. Others have begun HR Systems redesign at the outset of their projects.

Regardless, *failure to plan for transfer/sustainability is to plan for failure.* Transfer of new ways of operating and sustaining change will not happen by accident. The gravitational pull, particularly in times of leadership turnover, will be toward backsliding. You can easily prevent it!

Our concluding chapter looks at daunting organizational challenges that face leaders today—for which skillful managing of behavior can make all the difference. We'll take a behavioral view of challenges such as merger, acquisition, new strategies for top-line growth, and retaining top talent—and what you can do.

Highlighting Excellence . . .

Building a Culture of Leadership at Bechtel

An interview with Dr. Bill Redmon, Corporate Manager of Leadership and Development, Bechtel Corporation

"**B**echtel has built a legacy of leadership through its more than 100 years. In the early 1990s, Chairman & CEO Riley Bechtel began to build a formal leadership model known as Leadership 2001 that included specific expectations for leaders in terms of *be* (ethics and values), *know* (skills and knowledge), and *do* (specific actions to execute the model).

Several management development experiences were implemented during the decade to improve leadership skills and proficiency. Following introduction of the Leadership 2001 model in 1994, Bechtel initiated 360-degree development reviews when we first began working with CLG, and when the company really started to focus on feedback. That initiative grew into *Performance-Based Leadership*™ (PBL), and represented a shift from antecedents to consequences, with an emphasis on intensive executive coaching.

The PBL Story

We have been continuously improving and expanding the foundation for leadership as we move forward. For example, PBL has just been expanded to involve another 1,000 people in training and coaching, in addition to the nearly 1,200 who've already been through the process. More than 7,000 direct reports have participated in the upward feedback process. They receive orientation, provide feedback, and participate in dialogue sessions.

Also, we have used the PBL skills and practices to provide a foundation for other efforts, including Six Sigma, where behavior and process improvement were brought together in one approach. The master black belts are trained in PBL, and each process improvement plan includes a behavior change plan.

We also emphasize goal-setting and set explicit written goals for executive leaders across critical performance areas, including leadership. Performance against goals is scored, and the impact of each leader on the business is assessed and linked to compensation.

About five years ago, we stopped corporate funding of PBL as an initiative, but every business unit in the company continued to request and utilize executive coaching. The Chairman and other top leaders in the company all continue to participate in the coaching. PBL On-Line continues to be the most popular course on Bechtel University. And none of this is required on a company-wide basis.

People and leadership practices have been integrated into the company's executive decision-making. Every Operating Committee agenda now has "People & Leadership" as a standing item. An advisory group on people and leadership was established to provide input to the Operating Committee and COO on development, processes for succession planning, performance management, and related areas. PBL is embedded in the company's governance, demonstrating the power of consequences.

While senior management has clearly embraced the concept of Behavioral Science and performance, most of the next generation of leaders is already in coaching—they understand its importance. Clearly, PBL will remain an important part of this company going forward. In fact, we see PBL as the primary driver for supervisor engagement with employees, and as a key driver for employee satisfaction.

It Hasn't Always Been This Way

When I first arrived and was coaching senior executives, I had an appointment with one who was a known challenge in terms of his treatment of people. I arrived at his office, and his assistant asked me to wait, which I did I—for an hour—in fact, I waited the entire day, and he was still in a meeting. So I returned the following day, and he was still in a meeting.

Finally, he agreed to see me, and eventually got involved in the coaching. In fact, he became one of the most responsive in the company, because he came to see the value of leadership behavior and realized that the company was committed to it long-term—it's not just another "flavor of the month."

I tell that story because it is in direct contrast to what I see now in terms of demand-pull for more than 1,000 people in training and coaching. But it didn't happen automatically. We had sustained senior executive support from the beginning from people who walk the talk by participating in the development and coaching. At this point, I could schedule every day with training and coaching, and it still wouldn't cover the requests my office receives.

Tracking Success

We have tracked the success of many changes I mentioned using data from our employee satisfaction survey, 360 assessments, and leadership scorecards. The results are positive across the board. Our employee survey shows that "immediate supervisor" effectiveness has become a strength over the past five years. Our 360 assessments across all senior leaders show a positive upward trend over the past few years. And our leadership scorecard results show that employees feel their supervisors show improved leadership behavior following their PBL training and coaching.

Over the past year, we have leveraged PBL and our focus on behavior as part of a companywide talent strategy designed to ensure that we are world class in finding, developing, managing, and retaining our talent. High performance in these areas will ensure a long-term supply of the best talent for our business and provide the best teams in the industry to build projects in all of our market segments. Bechtel is committed to building and maintaining a culture of leadership—long-term and around the world.

I believe that our focus on leadership has led to significant business success. We've been the top-rated U.S. contractor for seven straight years by *Engineering News-Record* (ENR.com). It is not our explicit goal to be number 1, but our focus on leadership, safety, and quality help make us the leader in the industry."

Leading Through the Challenges of Today and Tomorrow

"When I entered the business world 25 years ago, things seemed much more straightforward. I was not in HR then, but might as well have been—I managed large groups of operators and ran large segments of the business. Even then, it was all about having the right people, well-trained, where and when you needed them.

"Now, it is much more complex. Our workforce is global— 50% outside the U.S. We face huge retirement numbers among our most knowledgeable and loyal workers at a time when those coming up are better-educated formally, but have less time-in-job and hands-on knowledge. Many have come from other companies and industries.

"Also, this younger generation is far more choiceful about work they are willing to do and willingness to relocate. No longer do 'the company's needs come first.' These folks expect to be part of decision-making and view employment as a partnership influenced heavily by their family needs and the season of their lives. Are there any openings for someone who simply wants to run a business?!"

—*Chief People Officer, Fortune 100 Company*

Today's leaders confront a kaleidoscope of business challenges: Globalization. Emerging markets. Increased environmental restrictions and liabilities. Instability in nations and entire regions. Changing demographics. Many retirees with fewer experienced people to fill their shoes. And technology fueling everything to a frenetic pace.

Through it all runs a common thread: people and their leadership. Nothing happens until people act, so behavior matters. And leadership has new importance through these intense periods of change and new strategies.

Some of the biggest challenges our clients face today include:

- Achieving sustained/predictable top-line growth
- Improving customer loyalty, retention, growth
- Boosting innovation across your organization
- Effectively and rapidly integrating cultures and organizations following mergers/acquisitions
- Excelling at executing your strategies
- Boosting employee engagement/retention
- Smoothing leadership transitions and accelerating the new leader and team to hit full stride
- Ensuring that strategic talent management truly results in well-developed leaders

The behavioral framework you have worked through in this book gives you important insights in reframing these challenges—and understanding what leaders can do to meet them.

Let us say up front that each of these topics deserves its own book—certainly more than a few paragraphs. However, I hope that by touching on them here, and by learning from the successes of other leaders who focused on behavior, you will gain new ideas and insights that will help you in your business.

ACHIEVING SUSTAINED/PREDICTABLE TOP-LINE GROWTH

Companies seek the holy grail to drive top-line growth—great leaders; motivated salespeople; new products; breakthrough insights in customer needs, wants, and trends. Private or publicly traded, an organization's growth is synonymous with health and future.

Sustainable, predictable growth generally comes from maintaining established market share while expanding through product or service innovation—or through better sales execution within an existing customer base into new geographies.

Regardless of the strategy, top-line growth ultimately comes down to behavior, execution, and leaders successfully unleashing employees' discretionary performance on true drivers of top-line growth.

In growth, everyone takes part. Grow from the core . . . sell more products at full price . . . increase share of purchases from existing customers. All of this requires a sales force and leadership team that is well-aligned, motivated, and that gets results the right way.

Track the Leading Indicators

A key way to ensure top-line growth and profitability is to track leading indicators—key measures—that indicate the health of each brand or business unit. These measures become criteria against which organizational performance can be tracked—and from which pinpointed behaviors can be identified and encouraged.

One client developed growth scorecards that encouraged improvement in the indicators shown in the "Growth Model" figure. Here they were tracking growth indicators on their key brands.

Growth Model
Business Unit Assessment

Business Unit: Example
Date:
Completed by:

	STATUS Current	GOAL In 6 Months	OWNER	SPECIAL NOTES	E/D	BY WHOM
Superior Value Consumer Proposition						
1. Consumer Preferred Products			Marketing Leader/ R&D Leader			
2. Consumer Preferred Packaging			Marketing Leader/ R&D Leader			
3. Reliable Quality			Marketing Leader/ R&D Leader			
4. Pricing that Delivers Superior Value			Marketing Leader/ R&D Leader			
5. Consumer Derived Innovation			Marketing Leader/ R&D Leader			
Building Brands						
1. Equity Keystones developed for key brands			Marketing Leader			
2. Effective Consumer Communication Plans in place			Marketing Leader			
2a. Proven Executions			Marketing Leader			
2b. Spend levels are right			Marketing Leader			
2c. Consistent across all consumer touchpoints			Marketing Leader			
2d. Consistent over time			Marketing Leader			
3. Superior Packaging Graphics			Marketing Leader			

Other examples of what you might track include cross-serving (across services or lines-of-business, field sales synergies post-merger, percent of sales calls made to new customers, etc.).

With a growth model like this, you have a succinct framework to mobilize the **MAKE-IT MODEL**. Growth by business unit is clearly the business opportunity. The scorecard gives you a framework to track progress on key measures that are tied to specific brands—and quickly intervene if you find performance lagging the target.

Whatever your tool, track *leading indicator behavioral measures* that are tied to top-line growth, because from there leaders can make certain they are taking steps to activate and consequate behaviors they need from the organization. And if behavioral data shows they are under-performing, specific actions can be identified and assigned accordingly.

Remember—leadership feedback and coaching, in addition to organizational consequences, are important to align with anything that matters to the business.

Work through the **MAKE-IT MODEL** to evaluate how best to drive top-line growth in your organization. As you saw earlier, the key to growth is to align leadership direction and actions with the most important focus areas for the business. Be sure that employees know the key behaviors they need to do—and that leaders are aware of whether the environment is encouraging (or not encouraging) those behaviors to occur.

IMPROVING CUSTOMER LOYALTY, RETENTION, GROWTH

To compete in the global marketplace and evolving e-commerce world, customer-facing organizations must be deliberate in how they strike a balance between transactional efficiency and the human touch. Research on customer loyalty by Ray Kordupleski[*] shows:

- Simply measuring customer satisfaction is a poor predictor of what's really important
- Customer satisfaction ≠ repurchasing or recommending
- Customers who are passionately loyal (or "extremely satisfied") are the only ones who repurchase reliably
- It is possible to identify and prioritize the key drivers of customer loyalty.

Customers routinely expect their needs and expectations to be exceeded. They have little tolerance for consequences for their purchasing behaviors to be anything less than **Encouraging, Immediate, Highly Important,** and **Likely.**

As a leader in a customer-facing business, you must understand the drivers that matter most to your customers, and ensure no variation in what drives consequences for purchasing.

---

[*] Ray Kordupleski, *Mastering Customer Value Management: The Art and Science of Creating Competitive Advantage.* Pinnaflex Educational Resources, Inc., 2003.

One of our clients, President of a consumer products company, was frustrated by his employees' customer service performance. To convey this, and pinpoint his expectations, he crafted the following letter. It is an example of giving constructive feedback to an entire organization, which is never easy to do well. Such instances must be carefully selected, and executed with care:

Dear Supply Chain Colleagues:

We have achieved great success together over the past four years, largely because we've built an organization of talented people who make their numbers, bring us new ideas to win, and work together as a high-performing team.

Since we began this journey together, I promised to be open and frank in our communication. In that vein, there is something troubling me, and I want to share my thoughts with you.

The topic is customer service—and the fact that we are not satisfying our customers very well. Bluntly, we have strained many of our customer relationships to their breaking point. Some *retailers have discontinued products*, canceled promotions, and many have put us in the penalty box.

We have worked so hard, for so long, to improve our standing in our customers eyes, and to put it all at risk is dangerous and wrong.

Through the first half of FY07, persistent issues of customer service, quality, and production have cost us more than $12 million in unplanned costs and lost business. These unexpected costs spread pain through the entire organization, in the form of canceled or scaled-down projects, limited investments in marketing and innovation, and diminished bonuses.

Beyond the bottom-line impact, service and quality issues— such as those we have seen this year on three core products— can also damage relationships with our customers for an extended period.

Customer relationships now mean more than ever. In the 1980s, 80% of our sales came from 30 customers. Today, *only 10 customers represent 70% of our business—and one*

customer alone represents 30%. The stakes are now higher at every decision point than they've ever been before. If we don't fulfill our service and quality pledges to these valued customers, we will not succeed.

Simply stated, we must improve our service behaviors and deliver right now. I have charged Rodney and the leadership of the Supply Chain organization with tackling these problems head-on. We had a tough, but honest conversation about the issues, my dissatisfaction, and immediate changes needed. I am open to whatever it takes to quickly and permanently institute the necessary fixes.

In the area of customer service, I recognize the problems are not the sole responsibility of the Supply Chain organization. I have challenged the executive leadership team to ensure that all functions in the organization work collaboratively to ensure their Supply Chain colleagues have the information and support they need to achieve our service goal.

As a first step, the team has initiated the *Competitive Advantage* program—a set of strategies that in part will re-orient the entire Supply Chain organization around customer-first behaviors.

The goals of this program:

- Achieve and sustain *99.5% right-the-first-time customer service*
- Drastically *reduce or eliminate product quality issues* that bleed us of resources, focus, and investment dollars.

You will be hearing more about *Competitive Advantage* in the coming days. However, this effort will not make an impact unless people at all levels of the organization—from the factory floor to my management board—(1) *deliver their commitments* to the organization, (2) *pay attention to the details,* and (3) focus on *meeting customer needs*.

I am asking every employee to exhibit "Customer First" behaviors in all that you do and say. This means:

- Using the phone or face-to-face contact to discuss issues, not email
- Instituting a sunset rule that all issues are addressed by day's end

- Speaking up about issues as they arise, so they can be quickly addressed
- Sharing when you have an idea to improve a process or solve a problem
- Asking yourself whether the choices you make are right for our customers and consumers.

As you have heard me say many times, our people are the reason behind our success. When we succeed, we all share in the rewards. But when issues arise, our people must take responsibility for tackling the problems and implementing solutions.

I remain confident we have the right team in place to overcome the obstacles that confront us. I am committed to doing just that. I am counting on each of you to do the same.

Competitive Advantage and its behavior changes begin today.

We need you on the team to win. We need behavior change that puts the customer's needs first. If we do that, we will win.

—Dave

This letter includes direct feedback about problem behaviors and their implications, while also specifying the different behaviors he expects from the organization. The business need is clearly identified. The metrics have been named. The desired behaviors have been well-pinpointed and described.

This letter is intended to act as a strong antecedent, along with other information about Competitive Advantage program mentioned in the letter.

The consequences are implied—but it will be key that Dave continues to communicate with this intensity as he recognizes and openly praises performance improvement.

Building customer loyalty, retention, and growth come down to managing behavior and using consequences well.

BOOSTING INNOVATION ACROSS YOUR ORGANIZATION

Innovation—in products, services, solutions to issues, healthcare, biomedicine, technology—tops executives' agendas. Innovation also tops the agendas of world leaders. The landscape is changing so quickly—and accelerating—that companies are challenged with how to achieve breakthroughs in innovation faster.

Fostering innovation is far too complex to treat respectfully and adequately here—but so much of it is behaviorally linked, that we must include it.

Most often, we see innovation challenges associated with front-end or back-end cycle times. Companies either seek new ideas/product innovations faster—or seek faster deployment from concept to implementation. One company engaged us to help change their culture. They wanted a culture that did more testing earlier and stopped working on a new idea/product when early testing suggested they should—this to avoid excessive front-end investment and lost time.

Whatever the unique need, every case involves the behavior of people—the decisions they make, the actions they take. It comes down to alignment of consequences with generating new ideas—suggesting or trying new approaches—and raising concerns about current products/approaches (flaws, etc.).

Employees must first believe that the organization and its leadership value innovation more than status quo. More important, when suggestions are offered, that behavior needs to be encouraged, listened to, and acted upon.

My colleague, Dr. Julie Smith, tells an interesting story about innovation from an engagement she led with a large gas utility . . .

> Previous attempts at innovation had failed, including suggestion systems and idea boards. My team and I discovered that management was unclear and misaligned on what constituted innovation, what kind of innovations were needed, and how best to get more ideas generated and considered for implementation.
>
> I helped them analyze the antecedents and consequences that drove innovative behaviors and found many (unintended) barriers to suggesting new approaches. They benchmarked other companies where processes to foster innovation had led to measurable improvements in the number of new ideas, or improvements in cycle time. In all cases, those companies had cultures where suggesting or implementing new approaches was valued and rewarded—by leadership and special reward/incentive systems.
>
> The company's leadership team and I identified the utility's specific needs for innovation in diversification, safety, and quality. They defined what would be considered innovative and eligible for reward/recognition. They worked with leadership to ensure those behaviors were encouraged. They also implemented an award program for employee innovation.
>
> Suggestions had to be implementable. They could be tangible (cost-saving or revenue-generating) or intangible (general benefit to company). Awards were financial, typically in the few-hundred-dollar range, up to $55,000. Both salaried and non-salaried employees were eligible, thus encouraging everyone to contribute ideas. And the company became the owner of all ideas submitted.
>
> In the program's first nine months, 65 employees (about 3%) submitted ideas, one-third from management and two-thirds from union members. Of 89 ideas, all received positive recognition and a dozen received awards. In this example, they pinpointed the key behaviors of making suggestions—specified what those looked like—and then ensured there were encouraging consequences tied to them.

They key to encouraging innovation is the same as with any other behavior: ensuring that the target performers understand clearly what is expected of them, ensuring there are leadership-provided consequences, and aligning and encouraging the desired behaviors associated with innovation.

This program led the way for a substantial cultural change across other key performance areas, once the leadership realized the power of the **MAKE-IT MODEL**.

EFFECTIVELY AND RAPIDLY INTEGRATING CULTURES AND ORGANIZATIONS FOLLOWING MERGERS/ACQUISITIONS

In 2006, M&A volume worldwide reached $4 trillion, surpassing the previous record of $3.3 trillion set in 2000, according to Dealogic, which analyzes global investment banking and systems. The trend is driven by a strong global economy, for one. Also, some CEOs are feeling a "buy or be bought" pressure, knowing they could lose their jobs if their companies are bought out.

Other causes are particular to a given company or industry. For example, GE is buying and selling parts of its businesses to reposition itself for undistracted global growth. Analysts say the U.S. airline industry must consolidate to boost profitability. And one of our company's Japanese clients is buying a competitor in the U.K. to gain market share in countries where they currently lack presence.

Regardless of the underlying strategy, what we know is that M&A activities are on the rise, with all of the concomitant cultural and performance challenges. The need to influence behavior and merging corporate cultures is critical.

According to The Conference Board, **75% of mergers and acquisitions fail** (*Across the Board,* May/June 2004). This is a worrisome statistic, albeit an understandable one. After all, the probability that two or more cultures have identical consequence histories or ways of doing things is virtually zero. Each company has a history of encouraging certain behaviors and not others—which is central to how work gets done everywhere. If you consider the challenges of integrating any two corporate cultures, it is no surprise that so many fail. So, from the moment of the merger announcement, the importance of leading well and managing behavior begins.

Any merger generates an avalanche of new documents that disclose legal and business due diligence about both companies. But these documents don't reveal the full picture—they don't disclose the depth of *cultural* differences or reveal how work gets done in each organization.

In other words, *merger documents rarely reveal the patterns of behavior* that have been shaped over decades by the systems and people within each organization. In a merger, the players abruptly change, consequence providers (a.k.a. leaders) are altered, and antecedents no longer align with the same consequences.

Result: the old conditions that allowed desirable behaviors to occur are changed, so behavior becomes less predictable, less reliable, and less aligned with what made the individual companies so successful prior to the merger.

From reading this book, you now understand why the consequences in two merging cultures are seldom consistent—in fact, normally very different. Without consistent behavior patterns, there is no "common" culture when two (or more) companies have come together. And so, subcultures persist and a new culture does not develop for years and years—while profits suffer.

Creating a New Culture?

Leaders can create a new culture and shape new behaviors by aligning antecedents (like a new vision statement) with desired behaviors, and by ensuring that leadership feedback and coaching actively encourages those behaviors. *Taking the time to do this work is where most mergers fall short.*

In the frenzy to get FTC approval and names plugged into organizational charts, and in the race to get results and meet operating targets, it is tempting to view "culture" as a distraction and a waste of time. Dedicated leaders, doing everything imaginable to hit pro forma targets, often forget that it is their leadership that most powerfully influences how their organizations perform.

Key actions for successful merger integrations include:

1. *Get the right people in the right roles, with clarity on business objectives, roles, developmental needs and measures of success.* In other words, take great care with your selection decisions and assignments. Make the antecedents clear and consistent to those individuals. Encourage new teams at all levels to work together and to review the critical results targets at their levels. Pinpoint key behaviors that need to occur for the results targets to be met.

2. *Invest leadership time to coach and deliver feedback on key behaviors needed to achieve those results.* Shape behaviors that are critical to the success of the organization—don't leave them up to chance! Use a framework like the *Shaping Opportunity Grid* (Chapter 6) to ensure that every leader interaction is leveraged as an opportunity to shape behavior.

3. *Steward business plans with oversight of performance-versus-plan.* Use this opportunity to track progress, reinforce success, remove barriers, and take corrective action.

4. *Ensure that consequence systems are aligned with the (new) behaviors* needed for business success/desired culture. Maintained/improved business results are especially key in a post-merger situation. Leaders need to actively coach and encourage desired behaviors, and the consequence systems need to reward them.

EXCELLING AT EXECUTING YOUR STRATEGIES

Success in today's world will come from leaders who can deftly and reliably execute their strategies quickly, well, and with measurable results. Managers and leaders must decide where to focus their efforts, where the human touch will make a difference.

- Leaders' time and focus is a precious resource—to be used thoughtfully and strategically.

- What you say and do as a leader not only gives tacit approval for others to replicate your behaviors, but also signals what is most important.

- What you spend time on matters . . . and if you are deploying a key strategy of importance to your organization, it is important that you be seen as actively involved, personally, *in* this strategy.

- People will look for indications that you are really committed to it—and will listen for words from you about it—and actions from you consistent with it.

Much senior executive time is spent on implementing change, executing strategies, and leading organizations through the *Make-Its*—over and over. As we have said many times, the leaders' role is vital to the success or failure of the strategy being implemented.

The pitfalls we most often see are:

- Lack of leadership's visible sponsorship and in-the-trenches support during implementation
- Lack of alignment and buy-in on what is being implemented and what success looks like (how it will be measured)
- Insufficient implementation planning for the change
- Insufficient communications
- Wrong people in key roles
- Leadership not knowing what they don't know

Underneath each of these are issues of behavior, leadership, thoughtful decision-making, and actively managing the performance of others. Execution of new strategies tests leadership as much as any single challenge.

Working through the **MAKE-IT MODEL** guides us thoughtfully through the stages that prompt us to consider these and other issues that underlie causes of execution failure.

Recognize that your time/focus/behaviors as a leader are perhaps the single most important determinant of strategy execution success or failure. Using the IMPACT framework and behavioral tools, you *won't* leave behavior change to chance.

BOOSTING EMPLOYEE ENGAGEMENT/RETENTION

The statistics on employee engagement are shocking. According to the *Gallup Management Journal's* semi-annual Employee Engagement Index:[*]

29% of employees are *actively engaged* in their jobs

54% are *not engaged*

17% are *actively <u>disengaged</u>*

Similar research by Watson Wyatt illustrates how engaged, committed employees significantly impact the bottom line. Their work showed that organizations which invest in creating a higher Human Capital Index (HCI) were far more likely to have greater shareholder return than organizations which scored a lower HCI (see figure).

---

[*]Steve Crabtree, "Getting Personal in the Workplace," *Gallup Management Journal,* June 10, 2004, © 2004 The Gallup Organization.

Five-Year Total Returns to Shareholders
(April 1996 – April 2001)

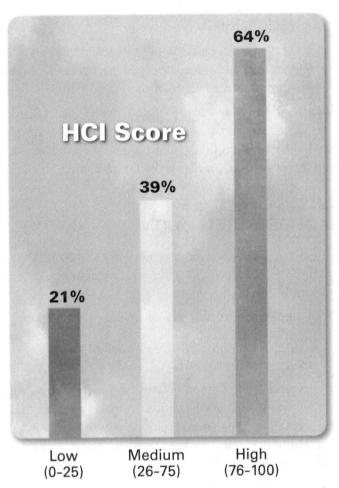

Low	Medium	High
(0-25)	(26-75)	(76-100)

Data: Ira Kay & Bruce Fau, Human Capital Index: Linking Human Capital to Shareholder Value, Watson Wyatt, 2000.

What is particularly interesting is that the highest area for creating shareholder value is *personal accountability*—in other words, *tying consequences to the behaviors of people and engaging them fully*. This is illustrated in this "key links" figure:

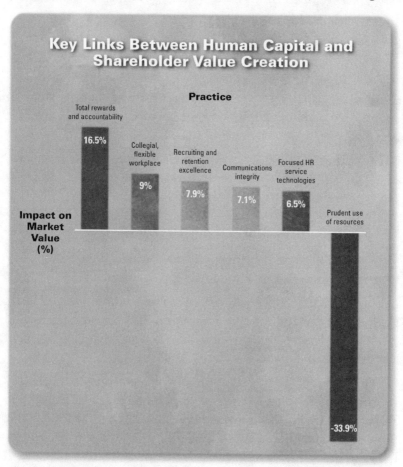

Data: Ira Kay & Bruce Fau, Human Capital Index: Linking Human Capital to Shareholder Value, Watson Wyatt, 2000. The figure shows the expected change in market value associated with one standard deviation improvement in the HCI dimension.

Research by John Kotter and James Heskett (*Corporate Culture & Performance,* Free Press, 1992) disclosed that over an eleven-year study period:

- *Average* organizations increased revenues by 166% and profits by 1%
- *Exceptional* organizations increased revenues by 682% and profits by 756%.

Jim Collins, in *Good to Great* (HarperCollins, 2001), shared research that spanned over 30 years. It showed that the stock of exceptional organizations out-performed that of average organizations by an average 6.9 times.

The business case is compelling: *organizations that have engaged employees (like sports teams that have engaged players) perform better than those who do not.*

Key Factors in Employee Engagement

So what did these organizations do so well? What are the key factors that most impact Employee Engagement?

My colleague Steve Jacobs, in collaboration with Charles Carnes and Mark Rhodes, has provided the research and thought leadership for our company on Employee Engagement and its drivers.

The following figure (Employee Engagement Model) shows factors that drive employee engagement. It categorizes them along company and employee dimensions: "Organization Value Provided" (meaningful work, rewards, etc.) and the "Employee Investment" (time, stress, etc.). All of these factors drive each employee's discretionary performance—in other words, engagement.

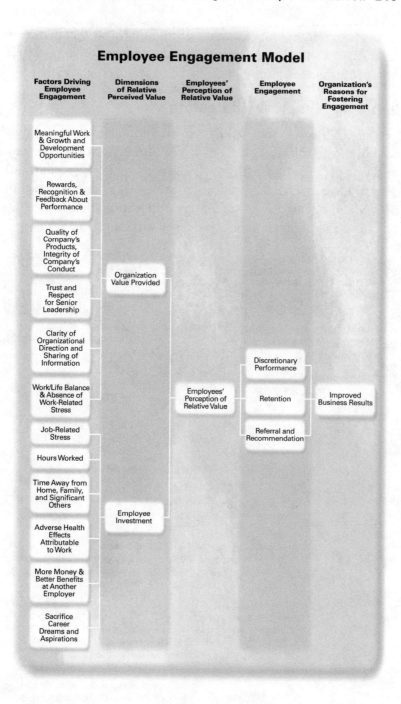

Employee Engagement Model

It is amazing how uncomplicated the items on this list are—how easy it can be to engage people meaningfully in work. These things are neither expensive nor out of reach.

Improving Employee Retention

The good news is that leadership can influence and improve employee commitment. In fact, leadership actions often have a faster, heavier impact than changes to policy/procedure or structural redesigns. The following table lists commonly identified commitment drivers and their implications for leadership practices and organizational systems or structure.

Commonly Identified Commitment Drivers	Implications for Leadership Practices	Implications for Organizational Systems and/or Design
Trust in leadership; values match manager's and company's	Leaders do what they say: actions match words Leaders' actions consistent with company's stated values Leaders treat employees fairly; clear expectations followed by consistent encouraging/ discouraging consequences	Organization defines values in meaningful, actionable terms Organization rewards behaviors consistent with values & identifies systemic conflicts Promotion/succession decisions pass "bulletin board test"
Recognition/ acknowledgement of efforts	Leaders "catch people doing it right" & encourage performance Leaders acknowledge those who demonstrate necessary actions *and* achieve desired outcomes Leaders develop custom encourager profiles for key players, then provide individualized motivation	Non-monetary award & recognition programs in place Fiscal incentives reward desired performance <u>and</u> outcomes Coaching & employee development seen as essential leadership function (linked to compensation & incentives)
Growth opportunities, challenging work	Leaders give employees "stretch assignments" with clear expectations and pathways, plus ongoing coaching & mentoring to ensure success	Organization identifies both assignments & individuals well-suited to "stretch"' responsibilities Employee development recognized & rewarded as valuable to organization

Commonly Identified Commitment Drivers	Implications for Leadership Practices	Implications for Organizational Systems and/or Design
Skills match demands of work; employees able to satisfy customers	Leaders use data, metrics, feedback to show employees that their actions impact customers & end-users Leaders provide training/ coaching to build skills & knowledge essential (based on data) to work & satisfying customers	Organization tracks and trends performance on customer satisfaction, loyalty, & internal surrogate measures Employee skills/needs assessments performed & correlated to customer feedback Customer feedback translated into training/coaching/ skill development plans
Pay & benefits commensurate with contribution	Employees receive frequent feedback on individual performance relative to expectations & group performance against goals Employees can access performance measures & understand linkage of daily activities to achieving business objectives Leaders conduct formal performance discussions 2–4 times/ year & summarize info during informal feedback sessions	Organization tracks & trends performance on individual & group dimensions Organization provides differentiated compensation relative to differentiated employee performance Leaders allow latitude to compensate outstanding performance by individuals or teams; give one-time performance bonuses
Policies/actions promote work-life balance	Leaders don't ask employees to do what they are unwilling to do themselves Leaders demonstrate flexibility to meet each employee's needs Leaders model how to balance work and non-work life	Organization provides flexible work arrangements Organization rewards leaders who model work-life balance

SMOOTHING LEADERSHIP TRANSITIONS AND ACCELERATING THE NEW LEADER AND TEAM TO HIT FULL STRIDE

Leadership of organizations has never been more in flux. According the Center for Creative Leadership, 40% of newly recruited senior managers fail and leave the organization within 18 months of their appointment. Many leaders will change their roles in the years to come, and statistics indicate that many will fail. But leadership transition failures can be avoided if success is engineered.

Our company's experience in this area is led by Hilary Potts, an expert in coaching senior executives through major leadership transitions. She and I have narrowed the success equation to ten key activities that ensure a leader's success in his/her new role:

1. Develop (fit-for-purpose) transition plan (both for your first 120 days and how you will lead thereafter)

2. Accelerate understanding of the business and organization, including history and strategic direction

3. Connect meaningfully with key stakeholders (boss, peers, direct reports); let them influence you

4. Ensure clarity of direction; create momentum for business performance

5. Follow through on commitments

6. Actively listen and communicate often

7. Model the teamwork you seek from others

8. Help change the people—or change the people (ensure you have the right team)

9. Manage the imbalance in your life

10. Proactively manage others through their transition

Following is some valuable guidance for each of these activities.

1. Develop (Fit-for-Purpose) Transition Plan

In the first several months of transition, your time is stretched extremely thin. You jump into meetings and the daily rush of business at a time when you are working hard to grasp what the business does, and how, plus your new role. Leaders who are planful about their focus and what information to gather can quickly discern facts and learn the business. The back-to-back meetings and daily business interactions become a terrific opportunity to learn the business quickly.

2. Accelerate Understanding of the Business and Organization, Including History & Strategic Direction

Systematic information-gathering and preparing questions in advance is more beneficial than meeting-hopping and playing fire chief. This systematic approach allows you to use the input, see a clear way forward, and articulate a strategic direction for communication to others.

3. Connect Meaningfully with Key Stakeholders (Boss, Peers, Direct Reports); Let Them Influence You

People will want to know more about you, how you work, and what you know about the business. And you should want to know them. Begin building credibility and connecting meaningfully with your direct reports, boss, and peers/networks from the outset. Ask their observations on key issues. Be a good listener. Answer their questions, and give them the chance to know you better. Through your words and actions, show that you care about them—and what they think.

4. Ensure Clarity of Direction; Create Momentum for Business Performance

People want to hear your expectations and the direction in which you will guide the business. Make certain everyone knows what success looks like—and what results and behaviors are most important to the business's success.

When new leaders come into a business, they may be unsure what they stand for, or the direction they want to take. A leader's first 2–3 months in this new role is the best time for a deep dive on the business. This allows the leader to really assess what's working and what isn't.

5. Follow Through on Commitments

Leaders want to be seen as making decisions and taking action. However, it is easy to get caught up in activities and make commitments you cannot keep. When leaders fail to follow through, others begin to question their intentions, and distrust grows. Our advice:

- Set expectations for the first six months, and revisit
- Be clear on how you wish to work with others (frequency of meetings; how you will exchange information back and forth; how you want problems/concerns raised with you)
- Write down the commitments you make, communicate them to your assistant, and be sure to follow through.

6. Actively Listen and Communicate Often

The key to leadership effectiveness is communication. Leaders who are planful about communications more effectively position their organizations to execute the activities that matter.

Your tone, tenor, and language are very important. (For example, see the masterpiece from Dave Moran to his supply chain colleagues earlier in this chapter). People listen carefully for clues and signals of your position, opinions, and style. Don't leave this to chance—always be clear through well-positioned communications, formal and informal.

Here are some tips for effective communications:

- Communicate through compelling messages.
- Hold discussions with key constituents (your boss, peer group, direct reports).

- Develop a specific action plan for engaging with others. Assess the quality and effectiveness of interactions when they happen.
- Align goals and objectives with your boss.
- Avoid the pitfall of unintentionally ignoring colleagues and peers.
- Assimilate with your team and set direction.

7. Model the Teamwork You Seek from Others

You may enter an organization that has an intact team, or you may have the opportunity to form your own. Either way, the team dynamics will change. People wonder: will our new leader have a positive or negative impact? Building credibility paves your way to gaining commitment and engagement. Effective leaders know the value of creating a high-performing team that can operate in the leader's absence. You can take advantage of your newness to develop a high-performing team or enhance the working relationships in an existing team.

8. Help Change the People—or Change the People (Ensure You Have the Right Team)

Transitions provide an opportunity to assess leadership talent, develop the talent you have, or bring in new people. First, though, ensure that existing talent is nourished and fully contributing . . . and we all know, that starts with great leadership from you.

9. Manage the Imbalance in Your Life

During leadership transition, your work and personal life will be out-of-balance, unavoidably. How you manage this will help or hinder your overall effectiveness. Whether you remain in the same location or must move your family, it will have an impact. This often comes when friends and family need you most. So, work this into your transition plan—plan for this imbalance. Help friends and family through this period by talking openly about it and maximizing your time with them.

10. Proactively Manage Others Through Their Transition

New people will come into your work group, your division, your accounts, your organization. Work with them to implement the transition effectively. Carry forth your learnings to them, and be a source of guidance and feedback, every step of the way. Don't leave their behaviors or success to chance. Proactively help them to win, just as you have done.

Managing through leadership transitions from one job to another, or one company to another, requires careful understanding and application of Behavioral Science, to benefit both yourself and the organization.

ENSURING THAT STRATEGIC TALENT MANAGEMENT TRULY RESULTS IN WELL-DEVELOPED LEADERS

Companies worldwide are struggling to "manage talent"—to find and keep strong leaders to handle the challenges of the current environment. But how companies actually find, develop, and manage talent has become stagnant. In a 2002 Conference Board study of 150 companies, only 34% reported that they could accurately identify future leaders in their business.

Between 2001 and 2002, forced turnover of U.S. CEOs increased by 70%. Many CEOs were let go for performance that previously would have been tolerated. But in 2001, CEOs were fired if their companies' performance lagged competitors' by 11.9%. In 2002, the axe fell on CEOs if performance lagged by just 6.2% (Booz Allen Hamilton, 2002).

The increased market intensity and demands on leaders arrive at a time when our population of potential leaders is declining. Stagnant hiring in the early 1980s has resulted in availability of fewer experienced leaders. And U.S. census data indicate that the population of potential leaders will continue to shrink for the next several years (The Conference Board, 2002).

In short, we have a challenging business environment and fewer experienced leaders to handle it. But these challenges also represent opportunities to fundamentally change and measurably improve how talent is managed. More than ever, we must treat talent management as an imperative, and bring it to the strategic planning table—where it belongs.

Without a Talent Plan, Business Strategy Is a False Promise

Whether starting new companies or preparing the leaders of tomorrow, the most successful companies hire great talent, make sure that talent is aligned with the company's strategy and culture, develop that talent aggressively, and reward that talent well, in alignment with their desired culture and future strategy.

A well-thought-out, documented, strategic *talent management plan* that brings together business strategy and talent strategy, is key. Business leaders and talent managers must see themselves as equal partners in business planning.

To manage talent effectively, organizations must do four things well:

1. *Align Business and Talent Strategies.* Make every aspect of the talent strategy link directly to the business strategy and its execution. (Anything not directly linked is probably working against the core strategy by consuming time and resources and confusing managers about what is most important.) Once the business plan is formulated, ask: "Are the current people processes ready to hire, develop, and manage leaders to support this business plan for the next 3–5 years?" Then, eliminate or adjust activities that do not clearly link to the new leadership requirements dictated by that strategy.

2. *Look Ahead, Not Behind.* Develop tomorrow's leaders for tomorrow's challenges. Talent management should be based on where the company is *going*, not where it has been.

3. *Track the Talent Profile.* Make talent metrics part of the business portfolio, with the same attention as other

bottom-line metrics. Talent metrics are not second-class measures—they are a vital part of your business portfolio and the best indicator of your future capacity to execute.

4. *Hold the Business Accountable.* No matter how brilliant the strategy, it takes people to execute it. It is too easy to be captivated by plans to secure additional market-share or tap new markets, but fail to ask: "Do we have the talent to get the job done?" "What will it take to ensure we have the talent we need?"

Require each business in the enterprise to provide a talent strategy commensurate with their operating plan for executing their business strategy. Without an equivalent talent plan, the business strategy becomes a false promise. Do not approve business plans that fail to address finding, developing, and managing talent to execute the strategy.

Continuing Flexibility Is the Answer to Turnover

Companies that view talent management as a hassle or annoyance miss the boat. Look upon it as a *recruiting and retention advantage,* and the light goes on! If you fail to match flexible arrangements to individual desires, you will neither attract nor retain top talent—people who, frankly, could work anywhere. You want them to choose you.

Day after day, employees must achieve a more reinforcing life with you than with another company. That's the secret—the behavioral secret—to keeping turnover low.

Further, sources of encouragement cannot be static. Your people's needs shift as they progress through the seasons of their lives, so you must maintain open communication with them. Good coaching and feedback skills will always be important. You need to regularly assess where your top employees are, and adjust each plan to maintain their long-term retention. This is particularly challenging in light of downsizing, which has affected most human resource organizations.

Like other challenges we've examined, overcoming the "brain drain" and becoming the top competitor for top talent is best addressed through Behavioral Science. To win and keep people, and sustain high levels of discretionary performance, the majority of consequences clearly must function as encouragement. It will no longer be simply a financial game—if it ever was.

It will come down to the motivational systems and encouragers that people experience within your organization. It will come down to having a want-to workplace in our have-to world. With the demographics and the needs of people in leadership roles, the have-to's won't cut it. Talented individuals will have more options than ever before as to where they want to work.

Epilogue

FROM READING THIS BOOK, I hope you feel renewed optimism about the importance of great leadership in all you do—and in all that you are. You are not alone to figure it all out. There is a science behind it all to guide you. And in all reality, you are likely doing many of these things already. Perhaps you just never knew there was a name for them!

Our world has never had greater threats, nor opportunities. So many of them come down to people . . . relationships . . . behavior. As you can now repeat to me: *Nothing changes until behaviors change.*

For most of us, success is determined by how well *others* do—those whose behaviors we impact directly or indirectly. We need to unlock their behaviors, if we want to unleash profits. It is up to us to engage the hearts and minds of people—and to unleash discretionary performance.

The **IMPACT MODEL** and the **MAKE-IT MODEL** provide simple, yet disciplined structures for us to change, understand, and influence individual or organizational behavior. *The energizing truth is: anyone can do it well, whether or not you were born with strong, intuitive people-skills.* Because it's a science, it is enduring and stands the test of time and trial. Learn it. Love it. Use it. Count on it. It will never fail you.

There is no better way to do this—reliably and with certainty—than by managing behavior thoughtfully and sincerely using the tools of Behavioral Science.

The first edition of this book was published in 2000. Today, as I write the second edition, I am told that it is the "reference manual" to which many turn, to solve their challenges of people and change implementation. So many readers have emailed me to say they saw themselves in the stories—or that they applied the methods herein to challenging relationships in their lives, and it worked.

I am grateful for those contacts and for the majority of readers from whom I will never hear . . . those of you who took away a nugget, a new idea, or a new approach that made a difference in your leadership, your organization, or your life.

We need to be the leader for others—that we seek leaders to be for us. We can make a difference through our words and actions—and arguably, they are probably our most powerful gifts. Feedback. Praise. Constructive feedback when things are not good enough. They are gifts we can freely give. They are gifts that affect people's careers and lives. They are gifts that matter.

Behavioral Science preceded us, and it will follow us. We each can make a difference along the way by learning and applying it consistently. I always say that I am still a work in progress . . . but ever grateful for the science and tools that guide me every step of the way.

I hope you have as much fun, and receive as many rewards in putting the science into action, as have my colleagues, our clients, and myself. Never underestimate the power of consequences. And most of all, never underestimate the power you have, or the effect of your actions on others.

Keep making a difference out there, and enjoy doing it.

£

About the Author

LESLIE WILK BRAKSICK, PH.D. is co-founder and Chairman of CLG (The Continuous Learning Group, Inc.), a consultancy headquartered in Pittsburgh, PA. As a nationally known consultant, executive coach, and author, Leslie led CLG as its CEO for over ten years as it grew to be the largest behaviorally based strategy execution firm in the United States.

Leslie's greatest strength lies in her ability to analyze complex organizational histories and challenging business conditions, and help senior executives articulate business objectives, develop targeted implementation strategies, and execute them successfully. Her unique skills and strong personal values touch those she works with both professionally and personally.

Leslie brings the same energy and skills to her many civic and community activities. She is a Board Trustee for Children's Hospital of Pittsburgh Foundation and Princeton Theological Seminary. She chaired the Women's Leadership Initiative for the United Way of Allegheny County (Pittsburgh) and has served as a Cabinet Member for the past three campaigns. She is an elder in The Presbyterian Church, Sewickley.

In 2006, Leslie received the prestigious *Athena Award* from the Allegheny Conference in recognition of excellence in professional and community leadership. In 2002, she was recognized as one of the top 50 business leaders in Pennsylvania, and was named a Carlow College *Woman of Spirit* and a Pittsburgh *Pacesetter in Business*.

Leslie holds a doctorate in Applied Behavioral Science and a master's in Industrial/Organization Psychology. She resides in Sewickley, PA, with Matthew, her husband of 16 years, and their wonderful children, Austin (12) and Madeleine (8).

About CLG

CLG (THE CONTINUOUS LEARNING GROUP, INC.), co-founded in 1993 by Drs. Leslie Braksick and Julie Smith, has grown into the largest behaviorally based management consulting firm in the world. CLG's clients come from the Fortune 500—along with non-U.S. clients of similar size.

CLG offers a consulting partnership that has a lifelong impact on its clients, their people, and their organizations. CLG achieves this by applying the science of behavior—which is the basis for this book—to clients' most pressing business challenges and opportunities.

Our consultants work comfortably side-by-side with leaders at all levels, in the trenches, sweating the same details of getting results that our clients do. We take time to build relationships that deliver results. CLG is an enterprise of uncommon people who perform uncommonly well.

For a decade and a half, CLG has helped clients achieve remarkable—and measurable—results in ways that also develop sturdy, positive, high-performing cultures. We help execute the behavioral portion of clients' most challenging strategies. Our clients turn to us whenever changing behavior, mindset, and emotional engagement are critical to achieving business results.

Please visit CLG at www.clg.com or call (800) 887–0011 ext. 2038 to learn more.

CLG and Intellectual Property in This Book

THE FOLLOWING INFORMATION is a continuation of the copyright page, identifying CLG intellectual property that is presented in this book.

- **CLG** is The Continuous Learning Group, 500 Cherrington Corporate Center, Suite 350, Pittsburgh, PA 15108, 412–269–7240, www.clg.com.

- The **IMPACT™ MODEL** is a trademark of CLG. It is a model for implementing change at the individual level.

- The **MAKE-IT™ MODEL** is a trademark of CLG. It is a model for implementing change at the organizational level.

- The **DCOM™ MODEL** for high-performing organizations is a trademark of CLG. It is a model for assessing organizational performance and potential.

- The **E-TIP Analysis™** model is a trademark of CLG. It is a model for analyzing the consequences of behavior along four parameters: Effect, Timing, Importance, Probability.

- The **NORMS OF OBJECTIVITY™** observational protocol is a trademark of CLG. It is a tool for guiding objective observation of behavior.

- The **Performance-Based Leadership™** (PBL) behavioral model is a trademark of CLG. It is a framework for behavioral leadership in organizations.

- The *Performance Catalyst*® process is a registered trademark of CLG. It is CLG's proprietary methodology for helping companies embed IMPACT skill sets across organizations.

Index

COMPANIES/ INDUSTRIES

PEOPLE